Essentials of Employment Law

Steven M. Bragg

AccountingTools®

Published by AccountingTools, Inc., Centennial, Colorado.

ISBN 978-1-64221-140-5

For more information about AccountingTools® products, visit our Web site at www.accountingtools.com.

Table of Contents

About the Author

Steven Bragg, CPA, has been the chief financial officer or controller of four companies, as well as a consulting manager at Ernst & Young. He received a master's degree in finance from Bentley College, an MBA from Babson College, and a Bachelor's degree in Economics from the University of Maine. He has been a two-time president of the Colorado Mountain Club, and is an avid alpine skier, mountain biker, and certified master diver. Mr. Bragg resides in Centennial, Colorado. He has written more than 300 books and courses, including *New Controller Guidebook*, *GAAP Guidebook*, and *Payroll Management*. He has also written the science fiction novel *Under an Autumn Sun*, first book in *The Auditors* trilogy.

Steven maintains the accountingtools.com web site, which contains continuing professional education courses, the Accounting Best Practices podcast, and thousands of articles on accounting subjects.

Chapter 1
Types of Employment

Introduction

There are many aspects to employment law, involving a broad range of topics – which we will address in subsequent chapters. However, a core concept that must be addressed first is the nature of a worker's employment with a business. Is a worker an employee or a contractor? What tests are applied to make this determination? And if the person is an employee, is he or she designated as an at-will employee, or is the person subject to a contractual employment agreement instead? These are critical issues, since many employment laws hinge upon whether a worker is an employee or not. In the following pages, we discuss how to make the correct determination.

Types of Employment

Employees can be classified as *term employees* when they are only being hired for a limited period of time, such as for the next six months. When an employer terminates the employment of a term employee without any stated cause and within the designated employment period, the employee can sue the employer for wrongful discharge. However, no damages can be claimed when the employer terminates a term employee for cause.

EXAMPLE

A rancher hires a sheep shearer for three months, which covers the sheep shearing season. The rancher terminates the shearer's employment after one month, which constitutes wrongful discharge. However, if the shearer had been discharged due to the theft of sheep wool, then the termination would have been for cause, so the shearer would not be able to sue for damages.

A more common employee designation is the *at-will employee*. Under this arrangement, either the employer or the employee can unilaterally terminate an employment relationship at any time and for any reason, unless there is an employment contract or tenure agreement in place. This arrangement means that an employee can be terminated at any time and for any reason by an employer. The employer does not even have to provide a reason for discharge. When this happens, the employee cannot sue for damages. However, some employment laws have limited the scope of the employment at-will concept. For example, an employer who fires a person based on race will be in violation of the Civil Rights Act of 1964.

There are a few exceptions to the at-will concept that provide some protection to employees. One exception arises when an employee is a member of a union; in this case, the employer has to follow specific procedures stated in its collective bargaining agreement with the union before it can terminate the employee. Another exception is a state-level prohibition against retaliatory dismissals when an employee files a workers' compensation claim. There are also state-level protections for whistleblowers who notify the authorities of wrongdoing occurring within a business.

Another exception to at-will employment was noted earlier, which is the existence of a contract between an employer and an employee. This contract should state the length of employment (through a specific date) or limit the circumstances under which an employer can discharge an employee. Such an employment contract should state the circumstances under which the employer can discharge an employee due to misconduct, in order to prevent slack or even egregious behavior by the employee.

Another exception to at-will employment arises when an employer does not employ a person in good faith. For example, a court would likely find against an employer that discharged an employee in order to prevent the person from vesting in a pension plan or accruing some other benefit.

It is generally quite difficult for a fired employee to assert claims based on oral employment contracts, since the employer likely perceives these conversations to be merely words of encouragement, such as saying that a worker's term of employment will be a long and productive one. Also, the fired employee must prove that he or she issued consideration in exchange for the verbal contract, such as foregoing work elsewhere in order to take a job with the employer. And finally, the employee must somehow prove what was originally promised, which may be difficult when the events took place several years in the past.

When there is a finding in favor of a discharged employee, the damages paid out are usually based on the concept of putting the injured employee in the same position that he or she would have been in if the person had not been fired. Typically, this means that the employer is liable for back pay and benefits that span the period from the termination date to the judgment date, minus any income earned by the employee during that period by obtaining employment in some reasonably comparable position elsewhere. Emotional distress awards and punitive damages are rarely awarded in these cases.

An employee can file a tort claim against an employer and possibly collect punitive damages when a wrongful discharge can be proven that is against public policy. These claims can succeed in the following four situations:

- *Refusing to commit an unlawful act.* This situation arises when an employee refuses to commit an unlawful act, such as throwing hazardous waste in a trash bin or lying to an EPA investigator.
- *Exercising a statutory right.* This situation arises when an employer fires employees for exercising their statutory rights, such as when an employee files a complaint regarding a workplace safety violation under the Occupational Safety and Health Act.
- *Fulfilling a public obligation.* This situation arises when an employee is fired for engaging in a public obligation, such as fulfilling jury duty or attending National Guard training.

- *Whistleblowing.* This situation arises when retaliation occurs against an employee for revealing wrongdoing occurring within a business. Whistleblower protections are included in several major federal statutes.

Contingent Workers

A *contingent worker* is someone who operates under a short-term employment arrangement, with no prospect of having long-term employment. Contingent workers include leased employees, independent contractors, part-time employees, and employees of temporary staffing agencies. These people have no job security, receive minimal training, and are paid no benefits.

Employers like to work with contingent workers, because it is so easy and cost-free to dismiss them when demand softens or the business needs to shift in another direction. Given the benefits to businesses of using contingent workers, it should be no surprise that there is continuing conflict over the rules mandating whether a worker should be classified as an employee or an independent contractor, as described next.

Employees vs. Independent Contractors

Employment law is intended to protect the rights of employees. It does not address the rights of contractors. In addition, the IRS requires employers to pay employment taxes on the compensation of their employees, but not any contractors that it may pay. Therefore, it makes sense for an employer to classify as many workers as possible as contractors. Since a worker's employment rights hinge on this employee vs. contractor designation, it should be no surprise that several tests have been developed to determine which designation should be assigned to a person. These tests are described in the following sub-sections. Their proper application has become increasingly contentious in an economy that employs a high proportion of service workers, many of whom are at least semi-autonomous, and so could be defined as either employees or independent contractors.

The Control Test

The control test is used by the IRS to determine whether someone is an employee or an independent contractor. The test requires one to review the entire working relationship between the employer and the worker, and arrive at a decision based on the complete body of evidence. There are three categories of facts to consider, which are[1]:

- *Behavioral control.* A person is an employee if the employer has the right to direct and control how the person does the task for which he was hired. The amount of control is based on the level of instruction regarding such issues as when and where to work, what equipment to use, which employees to use, where to buy supplies, what sequence of tasks to follow, and so forth.

---

[1] As noted in IRS Publication 15-A, *Employer's Supplemental Tax Guide*, Employee or Independent Contractor?

Behavioral control can include training by the employer to perform services in a particular way.

- *Financial control.* Facts indicative of financial control by the employer are the extent to which a worker is reimbursed for business expenses, the amount of investment by the worker in the business, the extent to which the worker sells his services to other parties, whether the amount paid to the person is based on time worked rather than for a work product, and whether the worker can participate in a profit or loss.
- *Type of relationship.* A person is more likely to be considered an independent contractor if there is a written contract describing the relationship of the parties, the employer does not provide benefits to the person, the relationship is not permanent, and the services performed are not a key aspect of the regular business of the employer.

EXAMPLE

Mr. David Stringer is a securities attorney who specializes in the issuance of bonds. He has been paid on an hourly basis for the last ten years by his sole client, Heavy Lift Corporation (HLC), and is reimbursed by HLC for expenses incurred. The CFO of HLC does not attempt to control the work habits of Mr. Stringer. There is no contract between the two parties; instead, Mr. Stringer simply issues an invoice to HLC at the end of each month, and the company pays it. HLC does not pay any benefits to Mr. Stringer. HLC is not in the business of selling bonds – it only does so periodically in order to raise capital.

The cumulative evidence in this situation is in favor of Mr. Stringer being an independent contractor. HLC does not exercise behavioral control, though there is some evidence of financial control that would be reduced if Mr. Stringer had any additional clients. The type of relationship is more firmly in favor of independent contractor status, since HLC does not pay benefits and Mr. Stringer's area of specialization is outside of the regular business of the company.

EXAMPLE

Myron Sotherby hires Ames Whitmore to supervise the construction of his new garage. Mr. Sotherby pays suppliers directly, carries workers' compensation coverage for Mr. Whitmore, supervises the work on a daily basis, and pays Mr. Whitmore on an hourly basis, irrespective of the status of the project. Mr. Whitmore cannot work on other projects until the garage has been completed. Mr. Whitmore is an employee of Mr. Sotherby.

EXAMPLE

Waylon Price has signed a contract with Milford Sound to provide concrete pouring services for several of Milford's public stadium projects. Under the terms of the contract, Mr. Price's firm will be paid a flat fee once specific tasks have been completed, and is liable for any subsequent issues with the concrete through a one-year warranty period. Mr. Price carries workers' compensation insurance for his business, and he employs several people. Mr. Price is an independent contractor.

EXAMPLE

Hubble Corporation lays off Red Miller, and then agrees to pay him a flat fee to design trajectory tracking software for one of Hubble's telescopes. Hubble does not provide Mr. Miller with any specific work instructions, and only sets a target date for delivery of the software. He is not required to attend any meetings of the programming department. He has signed an agreement with Hubble, which specifically states that he is an independent contractor, and will receive no benefits from the company. Mr. Miller is an independent contractor.

EXAMPLE

Vern Tucker is a paint specialist who works in the auto repair shop of a large auto sales company. He works a 40-hour week and is paid 40% of the amount billed to each customer. The auto sales company provides all of his equipment and paint supplies, and also monitors the time he takes in comparison to the estimates given to customers. Mr. Tucker is an employee.

EXAMPLE

Gene Brooks is a taxi cab driver. He pays Ultimate Cab Company $150 per day to rent a cab from it, which includes a sophisticated on-line dispatching service. Ultimate Cab also advertises its vehicles to the general public. Mr. Brooks pays for the ongoing servicing of the cab, as well as fuel. He keeps all fares that he receives from customers. Mr. Brooks is an independent contractor.

There are some concerns with the control test. First, it can yield indeterminate results, with some factors leading toward a worker having employee status, while other factors argue in favor of contractor status. Since the test includes no decisional criteria that state which factors carry a higher weighting, it can be difficult to come to a firm conclusion regarding a worker's status.

The Economic Realities Test

The economic realities test is used by the Fair Labor Standards Act (FLSA) to differentiate between an employee and a contractor. The intent of the test is to decide whether a worker is an employee, and therefore subject to the federal minimum wage and overtime rules. Someone using this test is seeking to determine whether, as a matter of economic reality, a worker is reliant on the hiring party to earn a living (which is an employee), or is self-reliant and independent (which is a contractor).

This test improves upon the control test in two ways. First, it can account for situations in which direct employer control may be absent from situations that would otherwise be classified as employment relationships, such as when a professional operates in a specialized field or the work requires a high degree of discretion. Second, the economic realities test focuses on economic dependency rather than control, so that workers are classified as employees when they are dependent on an employer, even though they might otherwise technically be classified as contractors.

5

The economic realities test is a multi-factor test, and includes the following factors:

- *Is the work an integral part of the employer's business?* If so, then the worker is probably classified as an employee. Conversely, if the work is tangential to the operations of the business, then the worker is more likely to be classified as a contractor. For example, someone providing plumbing services to an investment advisory firm is probably a contractor.
- *Does the worker's managerial skill affect the person's opportunity for profit or loss?* If so, then the worker is probably classified as a contractor, since contractors manage their own businesses. Conversely, an employee will make money irrespective of being able to use his or her managerial skill.
- *How does the worker's relative investment compare to the employer's investment?* A significant investment by the worker makes it more likely that the person is operating his or her own business, and so should be classified as a contractor.
- *Does the work require special skill or initiative?* An independent contractor is more likely to be trained and possess a special skill. Conversely, an unskilled worker, or someone requiring additional training, is more likely to be classified as an employee.
- *Is the relationship between the worker and employer indefinite or permanent?* A fixed, project-based relationship is characteristic of a contractor relationship, while an indefinite, ongoing relationship is more characteristic of an employment arrangement.
- *What is the nature and degree of the employer's control?* The level of control exercised by the employer over a worker is considered a minor part of the analysis.

In short, the economic realities test seeks to determine whether a worker is economically dependent on the employer or is operating a separate business. If the worker is economically dependent on the employer, then the individual should probably be classified as an employee. Conversely, if the worker runs his or her own business and is economically independent of the employer, then the worker should probably be classified as an independent contractor.

The Department of Labor has pointed out that an employer and worker cannot contractually agree to ignore the FLSA. Thus, if the test shows that an employment arrangement exists, then the parties cannot agree to ignore the minimum wage and overtime laws.

It is possible that an employer can manipulate the economic realities test to shift employees into the independent contractor classification, merely by adjusting the work circumstances of each employee until they qualify for contractor status under the multi-factor tests just described.

EXAMPLE

The International Sprinkler Blowout Company owns 20 air compressors, which it uses to send its employees around the local metropolitan area to blow out sprinkler systems prior to the onset of winter. Its workers are all classified as employees. The company owner wants to reclassify his staff as independent contractors, so he fires them, terminates their benefit plans, sells the compressors to his former employees, and then pays them a percentage of the sales they generate, rather than paying them a flat hourly rate.

The ABC Test

The ABC test is a somewhat simpler test than the control test and economic realities test. It is commonly used to determine whether a worker is an employee or an independent contractor in workers' compensation or unemployment compensation disputes. Under this test, a worker is considered to be an employee and not an independent contractor, unless:

    A. The individual is free from control and direction in connection with the performance of the service, both under the contract for the performance of service and in fact;
    B. The service is performed outside the usual course of the business of the employer; and
    C. The individual is customarily engaged in an independently established trade, occupation, profession, or business of the same nature as that involved in the service performed.

What this means is that a worker providing services is classified as an employee unless the person meets all three of the preceding requirements.

Employment Law Contractual Exclusions

Some employment rights cannot be waived. For example, a business might try to employ a core group of regular employees and a set of "contractors" who engage in the same work and report to the same managers. In this arrangement, the contractors have signed agreements stating that they will be paid more in exchange for a contractor designation and not receiving any benefits. The IRS has stated that this arrangement is not valid, on the grounds that the control test mandates that the "contractors" are actually employees.

    If an employer wants to obtain the benefits of using workers that are designated as contractors, then it must actually treat them as contractors. This means giving the workers control over how and where they conduct their work.

On-Demand Workers

In the on-demand economy, workers may be hired for just a few minutes (such as to deliver a meal from a restaurant to someone's home) or for a single drive (such as to drive a person from her home to the theater). These workers may take on a number of these very short-term arrangements within a single day. People working under these "gig" arrangements are more likely to be classified as independent contractors; as such, they have no protection under the various federal-level employment laws.

Summary

The preceding discussion has included a number of tests and examples that can be used to determine whether workers should be classified as employees or contractors. An employer should have a clear understanding of these concepts in order to decide whether the employment laws covered in the next chapter apply to them.

Chapter 2
Employment Laws

Introduction

The federal government has produced a veritable blizzard of employment laws over the years. In this chapter, we note the key features of these federal laws. In addition, an employer should examine all state-level employment laws that apply to its locations.

Covered Employers

The various employment laws exempt some employers from being subject to some or all aspects of the laws. There is no consistency between the laws in regard to which employers are covered. However, there is generally an exemption for small employers, which is usually defined by the number of employees. For example, the WARN Act (as discussed later) contains an exemption for employers with fewer than 100 employees, while the FMLA (as discussed later) contains an exemption for employers with fewer than 50 employees. The statutes issued by some states have lower exemption levels, so business owners need to be aware of these state-level requirements. Other coverage is based on sales levels. For example, the National Labor Relations Board's jurisdiction over retail businesses begins at firms having annual sales of at least $500,000. These exemptions are provided in order to reduce the paperwork requirements that would otherwise apply to smaller firms, which may give these entities a chance to grow.

A special situation arises when an employee leasing company hires workers and then leases them to another firm. The lessor pays all wages, payroll taxes, and benefits, while the lessee pays the lessor. This arrangement works well for small businesses, because the lessor can achieve significant economies of scale by employing thousands of people and then leveraging this worker base to obtain better rates from insurers. When a business leases its employees, the organization is still subject to all employment laws. This is because the lessee directs its workers in how to complete their tasks, and so is considered to be the employer.

Anti-Discrimination Laws

By far the largest cluster of labor laws addresses the concept of discrimination. The laws create protected groups that cannot be discriminated against. Over time, the number of these groups has expanded to include the concepts of age, disability, genetic predisposition, pregnancy, uniformed services, race, color, religion, sex, and national origin. A summarization of each law addressing these issues is noted in the following sub-sections. Many forms of discrimination are prohibited by these laws, including recruiting, hiring, compensation, transfers, promotions, layoffs and recalls, testing, training programs, and firing.

Age Discrimination in Employment Act (1967)

If an employer has at least 20 employees who worked at least 20 weeks in the current year or the preceding year, it cannot discriminate against the following classes of employees:

- Applicants for positions who are at least 40 years old
- Employees who are at least 40 years old

The discrimination concept is considered to include alterations to the terms and conditions of employment, as well as employment decisions. In addition, an employer cannot state age preferences in any job notices that it issues.

EXAMPLE

Norrona Software, a rapidly-growing software development firm, posts an online advertisement that reads, "We have job openings for young programmers who are willing to stay late to get the job done!" This advertisement is illegal, since it clearly states a preference for young applicants.

There are a number of exceptions to the Act, including BFOQs (see the Civil Rights Act later in this section), firefighters, police officers, certain executive positions, tenured employees, and employees discharged for just cause. When an employer wants to assert a BFOQ defense, it needs to prove that instituting an age limit is reasonably necessary, that the parties excluded from a job are in fact disqualified, or that excluded parties have a disqualifying trait that cannot be determined without knowing their age.

The Act also specifically prohibits any retaliation against an employee who opposes illegal age-related employment practices.

EXAMPLE

An employee sues Smithy Ironworks for age discrimination. The composition of the company's workforce is as follows:

- 35 employees work from 0 to 19 hours per week
- 10 employees work from 20 to 39 hours per week
- 5 employees work full time

Though the company employs a total of 50 people, only 15 of them apply to the definition used for the Age Discrimination in Employment Act, which is less than the 20 that must be present for the Act to apply.

In the absence of an exemption, an employer generally cannot force an employee to retire due to the person's age. However, it is acceptable to have a retirement plan that allows employees to choose early retirement as of a specified age, or at an age that they designate. Also, an employer can require retirement for certain employees who have worked in executive positions for at least the last two years, and who are at least 65 years old.

It is allowable for an employer to reduce the life insurance coverage provided to older workers, as long as the reduction does not exceed the increased cost of life insurance coverage for the age bracket in which an employee is located.

EXAMPLE

Adeline works for Monk Books, which makes presentation-grade copies of medieval books. Monk has a policy of paying for $50,000 of life insurance for its employees until they reach age 65. At that point, due to the very high cost of continuing the insurance, Monk reduces the insurance to match the insurance cost it incurred when the age of Adeline was 65. This means that her coverage declines to $40,000 once she reaches age 65, and then declines to $25,000 when she is 70 years old. This policy does not violate the Age Discrimination in Employment Act.

When an employer hires a person within five years of his or her normal retirement age, or after that normal retirement age, this person can be excluded from a defined benefit plan.

A willful violation of this Act can result in double damages.

> **Tip:** Under no circumstances should an interviewer, either directly or indirectly, ask a job applicant about his or her age.

Americans with Disabilities Act (1990)

This Act requires that employers accommodate the needs of job applicants and employees who have disabilities. A common example of compliance with this Act is wheelchair access to buildings and restrooms. Someone with a physical or mental impairment that substantially limits major life activities is considered to have a disability. Examples of disabilities are having to use a wheelchair, deafness, blindness, diabetes, arthritis, carpal tunnel syndrome, depression, and bipolar disorder. The Act also prohibits disability-based discrimination. Discrimination is considered to include all of the following:

- o Asking about the nature of a disability during an interview
- o Not considering a request to accommodate the needs of a disabled person
- o Refusal to hire a candidate based on a disability
- o Demotion or termination based on a disability
- o Harassment

EXAMPLE

Ellen is a manager, and is interviewing David for a position as a financial advisor. David is confined to a wheelchair. During the interview, Ellen asks whether David ended up in the wheelchair due to a car accident. Even though her inquiry may be purely due to curiosity, it is not relevant to the interview, and so should not have been asked. If David is denied employment, he could make a case that the question was evidence of discrimination in the hiring process.

To avoid the risk of discrimination charges as part of the interviewing process, an interviewer should limit all questions to such matters as whether applicants can fulfill the requirements of a job and the reasons why they left their previous place of employment.

If a person cannot meet the minimum education, skill, and knowledge requirements of a position, the provisions of the Act do not apply. That is, the discrimination concept only applies to those who are capable of performing in a position. An employer does not have an obligation to hire unqualified workers.

A key element of this Act is the concept of *reasonable accommodation*. It is defined as the removal of unnecessary barriers that restrict employment opportunities or prevent a qualified person from completing the essential elements of a job. A reasonable accommodation is not considered to be lowering the standards of a job or stripping away essential functions from a job. Examples of reasonable accommodation are modifying a work schedule to allow a diabetic person to monitor her blood sugar levels, providing wheelchair access to certain equipment on the production floor, and altering a job description to avoid heavy lifting. Reassignment to a different job may be an option, though only if the person is qualified for the new position.

Tip: Insert a note in the employee manual, stating the contact information for the person to be contacted about making a reasonable accommodation. Doing so centralizes requests with the person authorized to deal with them.

It is reasonable for an employer to make further inquiries of an employee who makes a request for accommodation. These inquiries are needed in order to more precisely determine the nature of the person's disability, so that the resulting accommodation can be tailored to deal with it. For example, the employer might inquire into the nature of a leg injury in order to determine how long an employee can stand on it, and what type of chair would be most comfortable for the person.

Note: It *is* acceptable to ask an applicant during a job interview whether he or she will need a reasonable accommodation in order to perform a job.

A request for accommodation can be legitimately denied if there would be *undue hardship* on the employer. This occurs when there would be an excessive burden on the employer, which depends on the cost of the accommodation and the financial resources of the employer. In essence, a larger employer is expected to have more resources, and so should be in a better position to provide reasonable accommodation to its employees. The reverse may be the case for a small employer, which may only have a few employees, and needs to have all of them deal with a broad range of activities.

> **Tip:** Before rejecting a request for reasonable accommodation, compile a list of alternatives that provide the same degree of accommodation, and see if any of these alternatives would be less expensive to install.

EXAMPLE

Sonja has a lower-back problem, and can no longer clean as many offices in her job as a cleaner. She requests an accommodation to reduce the number of offices that she cleans per day. This is not reasonable for her employer, who instead proposes that she be assigned all vacuuming tasks, so that she does not have to bend over or pick up furniture.

A particular concern for employers is a request for extended leave, typically to recuperate from an injury, when there is no firm return date. In this case, the employer needs to decide whether it can accommodate the relatively high degree of uncertainty associated with the request, where it will need to hold the position open for a potentially extended period of time. In cases where a job is quite specialized, the employer may have to reject the request, on the grounds that it needs to have the position filled at all times.

> **Note:** A request for reasonable accommodation is considered confidential information, and so should not be revealed to other parties.

A request for reasonable accommodation must be considered – it cannot be ignored. If ignored, this is considered discriminatory behavior.

> **Tip:** Document all requests for reasonable accommodation, to defend against any later claims that a request was not considered. Make note of all discussions with the employee, accommodation alternatives considered, and any parties consulted for advice.

In order to receive an accommodation, a disabled worker first has to request it. There is no obligation by an employer to infer that an accommodation is needed.

EXAMPLE

George works in the warehouse of Entwhistle Electric, which makes compact batteries for cell phones. He is shorter in one leg than the other, and so has difficulty walking around the warehouse, collecting batteries for orders. He could have asked for the use of a forklift, which the warehouse has in abundance, but did not. After a few months, his performance falls below standard, and he is discharged. George cannot complain that Entwhistle did not accommodate his disability, since he never told anyone about it.

The Act also mandates that disabled workers have an equal opportunity to apply for jobs, be promoted, and have equal access to benefits. In addition, the Act mandates that these workers not be harassed because of their disability.

Note: Medical examinations are not allowed until a conditional offer of employment has already been made to a job applicant. Also, if a medical examination is mandated, it must apply to all applicants to whom an offer of employment has been made – no one can be singled out for it.

Adverse action regarding a disabled employee is prohibited unless a condition exists that will prevent someone from performing the essential functions of a job. Thus, withdrawing a job offer because an applicant has diabetes, under the assumption that this person will require substantial sick leave, is not allowed. However, withdrawing a job offer from someone who has seizures is reasonable when that person would otherwise be in charge of shutting down a nuclear reactor in the event of a system overload. In the former case, the employer is making an assumption about applicant performance that may not be true. In the latter case, the applicant's condition presents a direct threat to the business, because a seizure could occur just when a system shutdown is needed.

The direct threat concept we just noted is a key concept when dealing with disabilities. An employer can reject a job applicant or discharge a current employee when the person poses a direct threat of harm, either to others or himself. The assessment of whether a direct threat exists is not based on generalized impressions about a person's condition, but rather on a specific assessment of an individual's ability to perform a job in a safe manner, based on objective evidence. The perceived threat must be serious and likely to occur, rather than low-probability and hypothetical in nature.

Note: An employer should not automatically assume that poor job performance by a disabled person is caused by the person's disability. Instead, consider handling the situation in accordance with the employer's normal performance review process, including verbal and written warnings.

EXAMPLE

Frank is a hemophiliac, whose blood clots very slowly when he is cut. He is trying out a new medication for it, which leaves him having difficulty concentrating for an hour or so after taking the medicine. Frank tells his supervisor, Lisa, about this issue. It is reasonable for Lisa to make inquiries about the situation, such as specifically when the drug is taken, and how long thereafter it impacts Frank's ability to concentrate.

Tip: Store employee medical information in a password-protected file, or a separate and locked cabinet. The intent is to maintain the highest possible level of secrecy regarding this information.

The illegal use of drugs by applicants or employees is not protected by the Act. This means that an employer does not have an obligation to hire an illegal drug user, or to continue employing one that has already been hired. Further, an employer is permitted to test employees for illegal drug use at any time, both prior to and during their employment.

However, the Act provides protection for drug or alcohol addicts for as long as they are considered to be in recovery. This "in recovery" status means that these individuals are no longer using drugs or alcohol. Though these parties are considered to have disabilities, an employer may certainly hold them to the same performance standards that it applies to everyone else. Thus, if an employer has a uniformly-applied rule that prohibits the consumption of alcohol on the premises, then it can discharge any employee that drinks alcohol on the premises.

If a discrimination charge is filed against an employer, the EEOC will send it a copy of the charge, and request that the employer provide it with a response. Supporting documentation should be provided. The EEOC will then investigate. If it finds that discrimination has occurred, it will give the employer a chance to settle the matter informally (perhaps through mediation). If this fails, the EEOC can file suit. Alternatively, if the EEOC does not find that discrimination has occurred or it elects not to file suit, then it will send a notice to the aggrieved party that it has a right to sue the employer within the next 90 days.

This Act applies to any business that has employed at least 15 people for at least 20 weeks in the current or preceding year.

Civil Rights Act (1964)

This Act prohibits employers from engaging in discrimination against applicants for jobs or employees based on their race, color, religion, sex, or national origin[2]. Discriminatory practices can include the areas of recruiting, hiring, compensation and

---

[2] A person's national origin includes the country or region from which he or she comes, or the country or region from which an ancestor came. A region can be identified as a group of people who have a common language or culture. Thus, discrimination exists when an employer refuses to hire someone because he comes from Lichtenstein.

benefits, work assignments, training, promotions, and conditions of employment. Under the Act, the following two practices are considered to be illegal:

- *Disparate treatment.* This practice occurs when job applicants or employees are treated differently, such as requiring an immigrant to take a language test when this is not required of a native person.
- *Disparate impact.* This is a practice that might initially seem fair, but which has an adverse impact on certain types of employees protected by the Act.

A business cannot engage in discriminatory behavior when advertising for a job position. For example, an employer may not insert any words or phrases into an advertisement that would tend to discourage members of a protected class from applying for a position. An example of a discriminatory job advertisement is, "Need detail-oriented women to edit manuscripts," as well as "Need robust young men to move furniture all day."

A business also cannot engage in recruitment practices that tend to discriminate against a protected group. This includes using recruitment practices that tend to block protected groups from being hired. For example, only hiring based on referrals from the existing staff will likely result in the composition of the employee base remaining unchanged for a long time. It is better to use a broad range of recruitment tools to attract candidates from protected groups.

> **Tip:** Consider developing a standard set of questions to ask all job applicants, and have clearly defined criteria for all positions. Doing so makes it easier to deal with all applicants in exactly the same manner.

The recruiting firms that a business hires to locate job candidates is not allowed to follow client requests not to recruit among certain protected groups. Thus, a recruiting agency cannot comply with a request to exclude Pakistani applicants, or not to hire Presbyterians.

> **Note:** A recruiting firm that does not take judicious steps to deal with a client's discriminatory behavior against the firm's employees could be held jointly liable for that behavior.

The Act also mandates that an employer cannot classify employees into categories that negatively impact their job opportunities. This means that an employer cannot funnel people in a protected class into a particular career path. Thus, an organization may not direct women toward in-house sales jobs, while men are encouraged to work in on-the-road sales positions. Doing so may limit the opportunities of the women parked in the in-house sales jobs, especially when promotions are based on experience with on-the-road sales. This does not mean that an employer is prohibited from concentrating employees with foreign language fluency in certain positions, such as customer service, since fluency is needed in these positions.

An employer is allowed to make employment decisions based on a person's accent, if his or her accent will materially interfere with job performance. This assessment depends on the specific characteristics of each job. For example, having a strong accent might preclude a person from having a customer service job, but should have little impact on that same person's ability to conduct research or design new products. Thus, a person's accent should only be an issue when effective oral communication is a key part of a job.

EXAMPLE

Sasha is a Russian immigrant with very good English writing skills, but she has a strong accent. She has a degree in biology, and so applies for a position at a local university for an adjunct professor of biology. The university turns down her application on the grounds that her accent may interfere with her effectiveness as a teacher. However, it offers her a position as a researcher in a biology lab run by one of the professors, since it mostly involves research work, rather than communications.

An employer is not allowed to discriminate based on its perceptions of how customers will react to seeing someone in a protected group working in certain positions. For example, an employer that provides field servicing for refrigerators cannot refuse to hire someone of Syrian origin, just because he does not think that customers will want him conducting refrigerator repairs in their homes.

An employer cannot slot employees into certain positions based on their national origin. For example, the owner of a high-end cupcake company watches lots of cooking competitions on television, and believes that only residents of England can make the best cupcakes. Accordingly, she offers a different position to an award-winning dessert chef from Slovakia, who has a lengthy history of producing some of the best cupcakes in the world. The same injunction applies to promotional opportunities, which cannot be restricted based on a person's national origin.

EXAMPLE

Dillon, who is Canadian, works in the accounting department of the Aggressive Collection Company (ACC). Dillon applies for a position in the company's collections department, but is rejected at once. Dillon, who has always dreamed about being a collector of bad debts, claims discrimination, on the grounds that Canadians are considered to be too nice to be effective collection agents. The EEOC investigates, and concludes that Dillon had significantly better qualifications than the two people who were most recently hired into the position. Further, the investigators find that the collections department has never hired a Canadian, even though people of this national background constitute 10% of the total employee base. The findings of the investigation conclude that ACC unlawfully rejected Dillon's request, due to his national origin.

An employer must apply its disciplinary rules in a consistent manner across the organization, in order to avoid charges of discriminatory behavior. A good way to do so is to set up and follow a detailed procedure for dealing with misconduct issues.

EXAMPLE

Mandy, who is from Haiti, works as a cashier at the Mulch Lawn Care Center. There are 10 cashiers working for the store. The firm suffers a decline in business, and Mandy is the only cashier who is laid off. The reason given for her selection is that she was the least accurate in ringing up sales. Mandy wonders if the real reason was discrimination based on her national origin, and so files a charge with the EEOC.

The EEOC's investigator finds that Mulch usually makes layoff decisions based on seniority, not performance. Mandy had two years more seniority than four other cashiers, and the entire group had the same performance reviews. Given these findings, the investigator concludes that Mulch used a false reason for laying off Mandy, and failed to follow its normal policy for conducting layoffs. As a result, the investigator concludes that Mulch violated the Civil Rights Act by laying off Mandy due to her national origin.

A further requirement of the Act is that no retaliatory actions can be taken against someone in a protected class who opposes discriminatory actions within the firm, or who files a discrimination claim. The prohibition is quite broad, covering any actions taken that have a retaliatory motive. For example, an employer is not allowed to make charges against a warehouse worker for the theft of inventory, just because he filed a discrimination claim.

Discrimination is also not allowed when an employee is associated with someone in a protected class. For example, it is not lawful to discriminate against a woman who gives birth to a mixed-race child, or who is married to someone in a protected class.

The Act also addresses the following issues:

- *Occupational waiver*. There are cases in which gender, religion, or national origin can be a valid requirement for a job. This is called a *Bona Fide Occupational Qualification* (BFOQ), and is essentially an exception from the prohibitions of the Act. For example, a business selling women's clothing can claim that being a female is a BFOQ for modeling its line of clothing.
- *Accommodation of beliefs*. If an employee has deeply held religious beliefs, the employer must accommodate them. For example, if a person requires prayer periods at certain times of the day, the employer should accommodate this need, perhaps by adopting flexible work scheduling. However, the employer does not need to provide an accommodation if it will impose an undue hardship. An undue hardship arises when an accommodation would call for more than a minor financial burden or impairs workplace safety. For example, a Buddhist monk who is also an excellent computer programmer insists on wearing traditional saffron robes to work. This constitutes an easy

accommodation of beliefs for the employer, since no financial burden is incurred by allowing the monk to wear robes.

EXAMPLE

Fireball Flight Services employs four people who are part of the Walhindra religion, which worships the spirits in walnut trees. These people request that they have two 15-minute breaks during the day to gather near the walnut tree on the company's front lawn to conduct prayer services. Doing so can be easily accomplished, since it only involves making some adjustments to the employee break schedule.

However, all four employees work in the company's flight support group, which monitors the company's planes while in flight. If a fifth person in this group were to also ask for the same break time for worship purposes, the company would have to deny the request, on the grounds that it does not have sufficient backup personnel on hand to continue monitoring all airplanes that are currently airborne.

- *Religious activities*. Employees cannot be required to participate in a religious activity as a condition of their employment with a firm. Thus, managers cannot impose their beliefs on employees, and cannot deny employment to people because of their religious beliefs (or lack thereof).
- *Harassment*. Sexual harassment is prohibited, as is any harassment on the basis of race. Examples of harassment include derogatory comments, verbal abuse, and ethnic slurs that interfere with a person's work or creates an intimidating work environment. Such a work environment exists when threatening and offensive conduct is frequently repeated, and when management does not shut down these actions.

EXAMPLE

Ali, a Muslim from India, works for a warehouse club as a forklift driver. His fellow employees routinely describe him using racist slurs rather than his name, and also yell at him in front of customers, stating that he routinely damages merchandise being brought out for sale. Management does nothing to correct these problems, despite numerous complaints by Ali. This treatment makes it extremely difficult for Ali to do his job. Given the frequency and severity of this treatment, a hostile work environment exists.

Tip: Immediate and appropriate attention by management when employees make harassment claims can significantly reduce the employer's risk of loss. It can help to repeatedly point out to employees that they should promptly notify management when harassment occurs, so that remedial action can be taken as promptly as possible.

EXAMPLE

Manuela, a Honduran immigrant, is subjected to an ongoing series of offensive comments by her immediate supervisor regarding her national origin. She has received training in the employer's procedures for reporting such behavior, but files no complaints with the designated member of management. After three months, the manager finally learns of the situation when Manuela's sister, who also works for the company, describes the problem. The manager immediately conducts an investigation and fires the supervisor. The employer is not liable for the harassment, since it took immediate corrective measures, and because Manuela failed to file a complaint.

- *Contract employees.* The provisions of the Act apply to not only the employees of a business, but also any contract workers provided by a third party.

Penalties for a violation of this Act can include reinstatement in a person's former position.

These provisions apply to any employer with at least 15 employees during at least 20 calendar weeks in the current or preceding year. However, it does not apply to any discriminatory actions taken by a religious organization that uses religion as the basis for the hiring or discharge of employees.

Consumer Credit Protection Act (1968)

This Act protects consumers from banks, credit card companies, and other lenders. Of particular interest is Title III of the Act, which allows creditors to obtain a court order to garnish the wages of an employee in order to obtain repayment. The Act does not allow an employer to fire an employee because the person's wages have been subjected to garnishments for any one debt.

Equal Pay Act (1963)

The Act prohibits discrimination based on sex for those tasks calling for substantially equal amounts of skill, effort, and responsibility, and where the working conditions are similar. Minor differences between two jobs will not impact a determination that they are substantially equal. When determining whether two jobs are equal, the emphasis is on the actual duties performed, and not job titles.

EXAMPLE

Mary is an audit senior who specializes in the auditing of inventory. She alleges that she is paid less than several male auditors. The male auditors being used as a basis of comparison specialize in auditing derivatives. Mary does not audit derivatives, and the male auditors do not audit inventory. Thus, even though everyone involved has the title of senior auditor, the differences in job tasks means that they cannot be compared for the purpose of finding a violation of the Equal Pay Act.

EXAMPLE

Verity takes over the job of chemical analyst at a food company from a man. Several months later, she learns that her pay is substantially lower than that of her predecessor, and so brings a claim of pay discrimination. Further analysis reveals that her predecessor had to conduct most of the chemical analyses using manual processes that required a great deal of skill. When Verity was hired, the company installed automated test equipment that made the work significantly easier to conduct, with less skill required. In this case, the jobs are not comparable, so Verity's claim will be denied.

EXAMPLE

Dolores is a credit analyst who works with David, who is another credit analyst. She learns that he earns $10,000 more than her, and so files a claim of pay discrimination. Further analysis reveals that their jobs are similar, but that David has greater responsibility; he approves credit requests from recurring customers, which Dolores does not do. This is a major issue, since their employer could lose a substantial amount of money if credit is incorrectly granted. Given the higher level of responsibility incorporated into David's job, their positions cannot be considered substantially equal.

EXAMPLE

Agnes is a warehouse worker in a meat packing facility. She files a pay discrimination claim, stating that warehouse workers in the company's cold storage facility are paid more than her. Further analysis reveals that the temperatures in the cold storage facility are maintained at a level well below freezing, which can cause physical problems for the people who work in it all day. The pay level for cold storage workers is higher than for the regular warehouse staff, due to the difficult working conditions. Women can apply for positions in the cold storage facility, and several women currently work there. Given the difference in working conditions, the jobs cannot be considered substantially equal.

EXAMPLE

Wilma is an insurance agent. She is hired into a new insurance firm, and soon learns that she is earning less than a male insurance agent who was hired at the same time. She files a pay discrimination claim over the issue. Further analysis reveals that the male agent brought several dozen clients with him to the firm, whereas Wilma did not. This revenue generation differential is a valid reason for the pay disparity.

Exceptions from the requirements of the Act are allowed when pay is based on the quantity or quality of work performed, seniority, or merit. A seniority system pays extra based on the length of a worker's employment, while a merit system pays extra based on exceptional performance. For these exceptions to be considered valid, an employer must have developed the underlying pay system without the intent to discriminate, and the system must have been applied consistently to all impacted employees.

EXAMPLE

Diane alleges that she is being paid less than another (male) payables clerk within the accounting department of a large company, because its merit pay system is skewed towards male employees. An investigation reveals that the payables manager had no quantitative basis upon which to award bonuses to employees, instead relying on his impression of who was doing a good job. It is apparent that the merit pay system is not valid, so Diane has a reasonable claim that her compensation level is unjustifiably low.

Note: The payment of a shift differential is not considered to be a violation of the Act, as long as both sexes have an equal opportunity to work on the shift with which the differential payment is associated, and there is a business purpose for paying the differential (typically to attract workers to an undesirable shift).

Here are several examples of situations in which the Act may be violated:

- An employer has 16 female employees who are paid an average of $52,000 per year. Men in similar positions are paid an average of $61,000 per year.
- An employer has 14 women on staff who all work in the testing department. It pays them at the 25th percentile of the pay levels indicated on a wage survey. Meanwhile, it pays men in all other positions at the 75th percentile of the pay levels indicated on the same wage survey.
- An employer hires 10 female workers and places them all in the role of assembly line worker. When jobs for more skilled positions come up, these workers are not selected for the skilled positions. This discriminatory promotion policy results in the wages of the female workers being artificially depressed.
- An employer refuses to hire women into outside sales positions, on the grounds that they are not aggressive enough to close deals with customers. Instead, they are routed into lower-paying positions on the administrative side of the business.
- An employer has eight salespeople on staff, of which one is female. The saleswoman receives a sales commission of 8% on each sale generated, while all seven of the salesmen receive a 12% sales commission.
- An employer pays a male production worker $35 per hour, and a female production worker in the same position $25 per hour, plus a quarterly bonus that is based on her meeting a product quality target. Since the female worker has to fulfill extra requirements in order to receive the same total amount of pay as her male counterpart, wage discrimination is present.
- An employer operates an occasional training program for its programming staff on how to program to avoid hacker incursions. Upon completion of the training, programmers are given a $1,000 boost in their pay. There is no evidence that women have ever been invited into the program, so they have a valid complaint that the program is causing an unwarranted pay differential.

- An employer has 20 women working as part-time customer service represent-atives, where they work for less than the hourly rate paid to full-time employ-ees. The employer discourages these workers from shifting into full-time po-sitions, and there is no record that they have ever done so.

In order to bring a valid claim against an employer under the Act, a worker must prove that a specific person of the opposite sex is actually earning more money while work-ing in a substantially equivalent position. It is not necessary to make this comparison between positions that are currently held at the same time. For example, a violation could be proven if a higher-paid male were to be replaced by a lower-paid female.

The Act prohibits any retaliation by an employer against employees who oppose the employer's violations of the Act, or who participate in the complaint process.

The damages for violating the Act include the payment of back pay and a com-pensation increase that makes up for the difference between the compensation of the claimant and the person used as a comparison.

This Act is broadly applicable to all businesses that engage in interstate com-merce, where their annual gross sales are $500,000 or more. Government agencies, health institutions, and educational institutions are covered by the Act, irrespective of their size. It is enforced by the Equal Employment Opportunity Commission.

Genetic Information Nondiscrimination Act (2008)

This Act makes it unlawful to discriminate based on an employee's genetic infor-mation or the genetic information of family members when making decisions about employment or the terms and conditions of employment. The Act also restricts the circumstances under which an employer can require genetic information about an em-ployee. When genetic information is obtained as part of a wellness program, the in-formation can only be shared with healthcare professionals; the information can only be provided to the employer in aggregate form. The intent of this Act is to keep infor-mation about possible diseases or disorders that is revealed through genetic testing from impacting a person's employment.

This Act applies to all entities having 15 or more employees.

Lilly Ledbetter Fair Pay Act (2009)

This Act is essentially designed to extend the statute of limitations for discrimination claims (which is usually 180 days). It does so by setting the start date for the filing of a discrimination claim as being whenever a person receives a compensation payment based on a discriminatory decision. Thus, a discriminatory decision that took place years in the past is still actionable for as long as the resulting reduction in pay is oc-curring.

EXAMPLE

Ms. Olivia Wilde is denied a promotion to a clothes designer position by Quest Clothiers, on the grounds that she is pregnant. Quest management then decides not to promote her on the grounds that she is responsible for taking care of the child. Ms. Wilde remains in her original position for the next five years. Because she is continuing to suffer from the lower pay associated with this discriminatory decision, she can continue to file a discrimination claim.

Older Workers Benefit Protection Act (1990)

The Act prohibits any age-based discrimination related to the benefit plans of employees who are at least 40 years old.

As part of an employment termination, an employer may have an employee sign a document, promising not to sue the employer for age discrimination. Such a document is typically signed in exchange for a severance payment. Under the Act, the following provisions apply to the waiver:

- *Consideration.* The waiver must be signed in exchange for valuable consideration paid to the employee.
- *Revocation and delay.* A person at least 40 years old can revoke this agreement within seven days of signing it. Also, the person has 21 days in which to sign the document. Further, if there is an employee termination program involving several terminations, this period expands to 45 days.
- *Written content.* The waiver must be in writing, advises the employee to seek legal advice before signing, and refers to rights and claims under the Age Discrimination in Employment Act.
- *Future rights.* The waiver cannot waive any rights or claims on the employer that may arise in the future.

This Act applies if an employer has 20 or more employees in each working day of at least 20 calendar weeks in the current or preceding year.

EXAMPLE

An employee sues the Red Herring Fish Company for age-related discrimination in the denial of benefits. Red Herring is a seasonal company that shuts down when the fishing season for herring ends. The company employed 80 people in the past year, but only for 12 weeks. During the remainder of the year, only a single caretaker employee is on staff to monitor the company's facilities. Given the short duration of the Red Herring work season, the dictates of the Older Workers Benefit Protection Act do not apply to it.

Pregnancy Discrimination Act (1978)

This Act prohibits an employer from not hiring or promoting a married or unmarried woman due to pregnancy or a related medical condition. In addition, the Act includes pregnant women in the same classification as employees with disabilities, which entitles them to the same workplace modifications and medical leave benefits to which employees with disabilities are entitled. The Act applies to any employer with 15 or more employees who work at least 20 weeks per year.

Uniformed Services Employment & Reemployment Rights Act (1994)

The general intent of this Act is to prohibit discrimination based on the military obligations of an employee. Key provisions of the Act are as follows:

- *Job protection.* A person's job is protected for up to five years while that person is on leave to fulfill military obligations[3]. This period is extended by two years when a person is hospitalized or convalescing due to disabilities suffered during the service period.
- *Job advancement.* When a person returns from military duty, he or she is to be reemployed in the position they would have attained if they had not been absent, with full seniority. If they are not qualified for it, then they are to be placed in an equivalent position for which they are qualified. The position given does not have to be the same one in which they were employed prior to their military service.
- *Job training.* The employer must provide returning employees with refresher training, in order to perform the essential tasks of the position to which they are assigned.
- *Accommodation of disabilities.* When an employee is disabled during the service period, the employer must make reasonable efforts to accommodate the disability in a position of equivalent seniority, status, and pay.
- *Health benefits.* If an employee's health plan coverage is set to terminate due to his or her absence for military service, the employee can elect to continue (and pay for) the coverage for the shorter of the service period or 24 months. For a service period of 30 days or less, the employees can only be charged their normal share of any health insurance premium.
- *Pension benefits.* When an employee is on leave to fulfill military obligations, there is no break in that person's service years for retirement plan calculations, and the employer is liable for all funding obligations incurred during that period.

There are several exemptions from the five-year limitation imposed by the Act. One is when the initial period of obligated service exceeds five years, which may occur for more technical positions. Another exemption arises when service members are involuntarily kept on active duty for a period longer than five years.

---

[3] The fulfillment of military obligations includes both active and inactive duty, full-time National Guard duty, funeral honors duty by reserve or National Guard members, and absences from work to determine one's fitness for the preceding duties.

> **Note:** The provisions of this Act apply to military service in times of both peace and war. It also applies to both voluntary and involuntary military service.

The provisions of the Act cover the members of all armed forces, including their reserve units.

There is an exemption from the requirements of the Act that is triggered when the employer's circumstances have declined since any employees left for military service. In this scenario, such as when there has been a substantial layoff, it would be unreasonable for the employer to hire back those employees, especially if they would otherwise have been included in the layoff.

The provisions of this Act represent the minimum benefit level that will be accorded to employees who also serve in the military. In cases where state-level legislation mandates lower benefit levels, the requirements outlined in this Act supersede the state-level requirements.

In order to qualify under the provisions of this Act, employees who also serve in the military must inform their employer (either in writing or orally) that they are leaving work in order to serve in the armed forces, and have subsequently been released from their service under honorable conditions. Formal notice is not required when it is impossible or unreasonable to do so, or military necessity mandates otherwise. They must also apply to their employer in a timely manner for reemployment. When the service period is up to 30 days, employees must report back to their employer on the next regularly scheduled workday. When the service period runs from 31 to 180 days, employees must apply for reemployment no more than 14 days following the completion of their service. When service was for a longer period, employees must apply for reemployment within 90 days of the completion of their service.

Remedies for violation of this Act are substantial, including reimbursement for back pay and lost benefits. These penalties are doubled if a violation was willful.

This Act applies to all employers, irrespective of the number of employees on their payrolls.

Anti-Discrimination Headcount Rules

Most of the preceding anti-discrimination laws take effect only once a certain employer headcount threshold is reached (usually 15 employees). This threshold figure is compiled by including all full-time, temporary, and part-time workers. In most cases, the threshold must be attained for each working day in each of at least 20 calendar weeks within the same calendar year. These weeks do not need to be consecutive. This threshold is most easily determined by examining an employer's payroll records.

Independent contractors are not counted as employees for the purpose of calculating anti-discrimination law headcount figures.

EXAMPLE

The Hail Correction Institute fixes hail damage, and currently employs 13 people. It recently entered into a contract with a local consulting firm to help it install insurance claim software that allows it to more quickly file hail damage claims with insurers. The installation is prolonged, because of the large number of interfaces that must be built to access several dozen insurer websites. The consulting firm puts two people on-site for 21 weeks to complete their assigned work. No one at the Institute supervises these consultants, who are paid on a milestone basis (by interface completed). The consultants are clearly independent contractors, and so should not be added to the headcount total for the firm, which remains at 13 employees.

Note: Many businesses routinely take on temporary workers from temporary staffing agencies. A business that pays for their services typically directs their work activities, and can ask the sourcing staffing agency to not bring them back. In this situation, both the business paying for their services and the temporary staffing agency can be considered their employer for the purpose of determining whether they are covered by the anti-discrimination laws.

The headcounts of two or more employers may be combined when they are classified as an integrated enterprise. This typically occurs when the operations of several businesses are so closely entwined that they can be classified as a single entity, such as when they share management teams, one person owns both entities, or labor relations policies are centrally devised. In this case, an anti-discrimination charge filed against one of these parties can be considered a liability of any entwined entity.

EXAMPLE

Universal Fiduciaries is a holding company that is solely owned by Alex. The company owns fiduciary businesses in seven states. Alex is the formal general manager of each of these subsidiaries, and regularly travels to each one to oversee how they are operated. Universal Fiduciaries provides all administrative services for the subsidiaries, including accounting, finance, insurance, and legal services. The finance services involve transferring excess funds from the subsidiaries to a central account, from which they are invested to maximize returns. Given these facts, Universal and its subsidiaries can be considered a single employer for the purpose of establishing a coverage threshold under the anti-discrimination laws.

A person who is a major shareholder, partner, officer, or member of a firm's board of directors is not classified as an employee. If a person is subject to the control of the employer, then he or she is classified as an employee.

EXAMPLE

Emily is a very senior design consultant. Since she is already at the top of the firm's pay scale, the management team decides to give her the title of partner, rather than a pay raise. She is still supervised by the firm's chief operating officer, and has no input into the strategic or tactical decisions of the firm. Based on this information, Emily is classified as an employee, and so is protected by the equal employment opportunity laws.

Anti-Discrimination Applicability to Foreign Firms

When a foreign employer is employing personnel within the territory of the United States, it will generally be covered by the anti-discrimination laws.

Anti-Discrimination Posting Requirements

A covered employer must post notices that are available to all employees, noting their rights under the various anti-discrimination laws enforced by the EEOC.

Anti-Discrimination Claim Processing

Once an employer has been notified that a discrimination claim has been filed, there are several ways in which the claim can be handled. The EEOC assigns a priority designation to a claim, depending on whether the initial facts indicate that the law has been broken. An investigation will then commence, involving requests for information, interviews, and site visits. Once an investigation begins, the EEOC can encourage the parties to settle the claim. Mediation may be offered, if both parties are interested in this approach. If the EEOC finds that there is evidence of discrimination, then both parties will be informed, and the EEOC will try to work with the employer to arrive at a remedy. If the employer does not agree to a remedy, then the EEOC can elect to bring suit in federal court. If the EEOC elects not to continue the case at any time, it issues a notice that closes the case. If the EEOC elects not to pursue a case, it issues the claimant a notice that gives the person 90 days in which to file a lawsuit against the employer.

Anti-Discrimination Remedies

There are several possible remedies that the EEOC can discuss with an employer to settle a claim. They can include reinstating or promoting someone, or providing the person with sufficient back pay to offset the losses caused by discrimination. In addition, the employer may need to pay court costs, the fees of expert witnesses, and attorneys' fees. When the EEOC determines that an employer engaged in intentional discrimination, it can also push for punitive damages, as well as damages related to mental anguish and inconvenience. Punitive damages cannot be applied to federal, state, or local governments.

In addition to the largely monetary payments just noted, an employer may be required to take a variety of corrective actions to eliminate the source of its discriminatory behavior, so that any chances of recurrence are minimized.

Consolidated Omnibus Budget Reconciliation Act (1986)

The key point of this Act (COBRA) is that terminated employees can pay for an extension of their existing medical insurance coverage for an additional 18 months. An employer must notify terminated employees of this coverage if they have at least 20 employees. Key provisions of COBRA coverage are:

- *Notification.* When employees become eligible for COBRA coverage, the employer must notify them of their COBRA rights. Covered individuals have up to 60 days from this notification date to decide whether they want COBRA coverage.
- *Duration.* COBRA coverage is 18 months when there is a voluntary or involuntary termination of employment or when working hours are reduced. If an employee is disabled at the time of termination or reduction in work hours, the number of months of coverage increases to 29 months. In a few other cases, the duration can increase to 36 months. An employee terminated for gross misconduct has no access to COBRA coverage.
- *Termination.* COBRA coverage ends when a covered person does not pay a premium within a designated time period, the employer ceases operations, the employer no longer provides health insurance coverage, or the covered person gains coverage under some other health insurance plan.
- *Fee.* The employer can charge as much as a 2% administration fee to former employees for handling the medical insurance paperwork on their behalf.

Employee Retirement Income Security Act (1974)

This Act (ERISA) is applicable to any entity that offers a retirement plan to its employees. Its key provisions are:

- *Exclusions.* Employees cannot be excluded from the plan if they are more than 21 years old.
- *Defined benefit plan funding.* If a plan defines the benefits to be received, the plan must be funded at least annually, and must be based on the amount of future obligations owed by the employer.
- *Company stock limitation.* The assets invested in a defined benefit plan are capped at a 10% investment in company stock. A defined contribution plan can include company stock as an investment option.
- *Cliff vesting.* The employer's matching of employee contributions, as well as other employer contributions to the plan, must vest after no more than five years.
- *Graded vesting.* Graded vesting is permitted, where employees are gradually vested in the employer's matching of employee contributions, as well as other employer contributions to the plan. There are minimum vesting levels per year.
- *Employee contribution vesting.* Employee contributions to a plan must be vested at once.

- *Insurance*. The employer must pay into the government insurance fund that protects employees from the dissolution of their pension plan.
- *Administration standards*. The people administering the pension plan must meet ERISA requirements.
- *Reporting*. An annual report of the plan status must be filed with the government. Also, employees must be informed of the status of their pension assets, as well as their rights under the plan.

Fair Labor Standards Act (1938)

The Fair Labor Standards Act (FLSA) originated the minimum wage concept, as well as the criteria under which overtime must be paid. The Act also restricts the circumstances under which minors can be employed and regulates those situations in which it is allowable to employ them. The Act applies to nearly all employers with sales exceeding $500,000[4]. Key provisions (as updated over time) are noted in the following sub-sections.

Minimum Wage

A covered worker is at least entitled to the federal minimum wage, which is currently set at $7.25 per hour. Examples of the types of workers to whom the minimum wage requirement does not apply include full-time students, student-learners, and tipped employees. Bonuses are not considered in the derivation of a person's minimum wage. Also, an employer can pay an employee who is under 20 years of age $4.25 per hour for the first 90 calendar days of his or her employment.[5]

> **Note:** Bonuses are not considered part of an employee's regular pay when they are made at the discretion of the employer and are not part of the employee's expected compensation. However, a bonus that is paid frequently enough to become part of an employee's expected compensation is included in the calculation of the regular pay rate.

EXAMPLE

Andy's dairy business is subject to the FLSA. He employs 22 people, all of whom are paid the minimum wage. In addition, Andy gives a $250 bonus payment to each employee just prior to the Thanksgiving holiday. He cannot use the amount of this bonus to reduce the hourly rate paid to a level below the minimum wage.

---

[4] The FLSA also covers hospitals, institutions that care for the sick, most types of schools, and government agencies, irrespective of the dollar volume of business conducted.
[5] The reason for the low initial minimum wage rate for those under 20 years of age is to keep them from being rejected for jobs, since they have fewer skills and experience than older workers.

EXAMPLE

The Rest Hotel requires its night clerk to sleep on the premises. The value of this in-kind benefit is not included in the calculation of the wages of the night clerk, since sleeping on the premises is for the benefit of the employer, not the employee.

Piece Rate Pay

Employers may pay employees based on the number of units produced, as long as the amount paid does not drop below the minimum wage.

EXAMPLE

The Antique Couch Company uses teams of production workers to manufacture its Victorian era couches. The team members are paid a piece rate that is a percentage of the sale price of each couch produced, minus a charge for any rejections by customers. Over the course of a typical week, the average team member earns $24.00 per hour. In a few cases of low performance (typically from new teams), the piece rate can drop below the minimum wage. In these cases, the human resources department has a procedure to top up their wages to ensure that the minimum wage is always paid.

Tipped Employee Compensation

Someone classified as a tipped employee receives at least $30 of tips per month. Employers are only required to pay tipped employees $2.13/hour, as long as that amount, plus tips, equals the federal minimum wage. When this is not the case, the employer must pay the difference.

Overtime

A covered worker is entitled to overtime pay of at least 1.5x the standard pay rate for any hours *actually worked* (therefore not including holiday hours paid) over 40 hours per week. There is no FLSA requirement that overtime be paid on a weekend, holiday, or other day if the total hours worked by an employee do not exceed 40 hours within a designated work week. The overtime provision is intended to encourage employers to hire more staff, rather than forcing existing employees to work longer hours.

Note: Individual state governments may apply more stringent overtime requirements, such as applying it whenever someone works more than eight hours in a day.

EXAMPLE

Evan, a security guard, worked 50 hours in his most recent week of employment, at a base rate of $15 per hour. Since he is entitled to 1.5x his base rate for all hours worked over 40 hours, he should be paid $600 for the first 40 hours worked and $225 for the next 10 hours worked, for a total of $825.

The determination of whether an employee is not entitled to overtime payments depends on a two-part test. First, the person must be paid a salary. And second, if the person *is* paid a salary, then he or she must engage in a specific list of duties pertaining to either an executive, administrative, or professional role (as described later in the Exemptions sub-section). A highly-compensated employee (one who earns at least $107,432) only has to perform one of the duties associated with one of these classifications in order to be classified as exempt from overtime. These tests are known as the salary basis test and the duties test. If both tests are not satisfied, then an employee is eligible for overtime pay.

Note: Any evidence that a salaried worker is financially penalized for routine disciplinary matters can result in the person being classified as an hourly worker. When this is the case, every employee in the same classification who works for the same manager will also be classified as an hourly worker.

Waiting for Work

An employer that requires its employees to be at work is required to pay for this time, even if the employee is doing nothing.

EXAMPLE

Sarah is a ski patroller. She is required by the ski area that employs her to be on the job at 7:30 a.m. during ski season, even though the chairlifts do not begin transporting skiers up the mountain until an hour later. Sarah is entitled to compensation for this period, since the ski area requires her to be present.

Pay Periods Not Covered

The FLSA does not mandate any payments for time off, such as for sick time, holiday time, or vacation time.

EXAMPLE

One Year Corporation (which reflects the average tenure of its employees) offers its employees no vacation or sick time at all, on the grounds that all hours worked are billable to clients, and the staff gets a share of the company's profits. If they want time off, they should "go work for a wimpy competitor," in the immortal words of the company president. This time-off policy does not violate the FMLA, though it could run afoul of applicable state laws.

Exemptions

Exemptions from the minimum wage and overtime provisions of the Act are provided for those in executive, professional, administrative, creative professional, computer, and outside sales positions. More specifically:

o *Exempted executive position.* The person must be paid more than a predetermined threshold level, be responsible for at least managing a department, direct the work of at least two other employees, and have the authority to hire or fire other employees.

o *Exempted professional position.* The person must be paid more than a predetermined threshold level, and perform work requiring advanced knowledge in a field of science or learning that required a prolonged course of specialized instruction. The knowledge must be in a field that is similar to law, medicine, accounting, theology, teaching, engineering, and other sciences. A skilled trade is not considered to fall within these classifications.

o *Exempted administrative position.* The person must be paid more than a predetermined threshold level, be responsible for the performance of office or non-manual work directly related to the business operations of the employer, and have the duty to exercise discretion and independent judgment concerning matters of significance.

o *Exempted creative professional position.* The person must be paid more than a predetermined threshold level, and be primarily engaged in performing work requiring imagination, invention, talent or originality in a creative or artistic field. Examples of positions classified as creative professional include actors, musicians, composers, writers, cartoonists, and painters.

o *Exempted computer position.* The person must be paid more than a predetermined threshold level, be employed as computer systems analyst, programmer, or software engineer, and be engaged in systems analysis, system implementations, or system modifications.

o *Exempted outside sales position.* The person's primary duty must be generating sales, and the person must be regularly engaged away from the employer's place of business.

o *Exempted highly compensated employees.* The person must be paid at least $107,432, perform office or non-manual work, and routinely perform one or more of the duties of an exempt administrative, executive, or professional employee noted earlier.

Blue collar positions are always covered by the Act, no matter how highly-paid they may be. This group includes fire fighters, police officers, highway patrol officers, park rangers, paramedics, rescue workers, probation officers, and those in similar positions.

Child Labor

When there is child labor, their hours are restricted and the work environment must not jeopardize their health. The exact restrictions vary by industry. The minimum age for most types of non-farm employment is 16, though up to two years younger is allowed in some cases, with significant restrictions on daily working hours[6]. Exemptions from all age restrictions are provided for entertainment performances, working for parents in certain non-farm businesses, and delivering newspapers. The Department of Labor can set a minimum age of 18 for work that it considers to be especially hazardous. Individual states have enacted many variations on these restrictions and exemptions.

Home Work

A business cannot have employees work on the manufacture of a variety of items from home, such as embroideries, gloves and mittens, and jewelry, without the prior agreement of the Department of Labor.

Firing Restrictions

An employer cannot fire or discriminate against an employee who has filed a complaint against the organization.

Posted Information

The employer must make employees aware of the provisions of this Act by posting the relevant information in a public area. A poster containing this information is available from the Wage and Hour Division.

Employee Information

The employer is required to store a variety of information about employees for a period of two to three years[7]. The data to be stored for each employee includes the following:

- o   Full name
- o   Address
- o   Social security number
- o   Birth date
- o   Occupation
- o   Sex
- o   Basis on which wages are paid (such as dollars per hour, week, or month)
- o   Date of each wage payment and the pay period covered by it
- o   Additions to employee pay
- o   Deductions from employee pay
- o   Hours worked each day

---

[6] The restrictions on work for those 14 to 15 years old is capped at three hours on a school day or 18 hours in a school week, as well as eight hours on a non-school day or 40 hours in a non-school week. Generally, work hours must be between 7 a.m. and 7 p.m.

[7] Payroll records, sales and purchase records, and collective bargaining agreements must be retained for at least three years. Wage computation records should be retained for at least two years.

- o Normal hourly rate of pay
- o Starting time and day of workweek
- o Total hours worked each week
- o Total straight-time daily or weekly earnings
- o Total wages paid in each pay period
- o Total workweek overtime earnings

Any timekeeping format is acceptable. A sample timecard appears in the following exhibit that could be used. A timecard is usually printed on heavier-weight paper and is stored in a central timecard rack. Employees can fill it out by hand, or they can insert it into a punch clock, which stamps the time on it. There are separate columns for the beginning and ending times when regular hours and overtime hours are worked. There is also a small block next to each day of regular and overtime hours, in which the payroll staff enters the total time worked for that day. They then accumulate these daily totals into overtime and regular time totals at the bottom of the timecard. Both the employee and his or her supervisor should sign the card.

Sample Timecard

Overtime				Regular Time	
		1st Day	IN		
			OUT		
		2nd Day	IN		
			OUT		
		3rd Day	IN		
			OUT		
		4th Day	IN		
			OUT		
		5th Day	IN		
			OUT		
		6th Day	IN		
			OUT		
		7th Day	IN		
			OUT		

Timecard

Employee Name

Overtime Total

Regular Time Total

Employee Signature Block

Supervisor Signature Block

The timesheet differs from the timecard in that there is no provision for a time stamp by a punch clock. Instead, employees are expected to fill out the timesheet by hand. This is a relatively simple document, as illustrated in the following sample. Employees state the time period worked and the number and types of hours worked. There is also space for supervisory approval of the document. The name of the supervisor is stated near the top of the form, in case the payroll staff wants to contact that person with a question about information on the timesheet.

Sample Weekly Timesheet

Weekly Timesheet

| Employee Name |
| Supervisor Name |
| Week of ____ to ____ |

Day	Regular	Overtime	Vacation	Sick	Holiday	Leave	Other	Total
				Hours				
Monday								
Tuesday								
Wednesday								
Thursday								
Friday								
Saturday								
Sunday								
Total Hours								

| Employee Signature |
| Supervisor Signature |

When employees work on a schedule that rarely varies, it is acceptable to record the person's time on an exception basis when he or she varies from the normal schedule.

Enforcement

The Wage and Hour Division of the Department of Labor is responsible for the administration and enforcement of the Fair Labor Standards Act, though the U.S. Office of Personnel Management does so for certain federal employees.

Best Practice: To avoid running afoul of the provisions of the FLSA, do not try to classify employees as salaried in order to avoid paying overtime.

Family and Medical Leave Act (1993)

If an employer has at least 50 employees during at least 20 calendar work weeks of the current or preceding year, the Family and Medical Leave Act (FMLA) allows its employees to take up to 12 unpaid weeks of leave for a variety of reasons related to family and medical issues. Key reasons supporting a leave of absence are:

- Birth of a child
- Placement with the employee of a child for adoption or foster care
- Caring for a family member[8] who has a serious illness
- Having a serious illness that renders the employee unable to perform his or her job

The leave period is extended to 26 weeks when caring for a family member in military service with a serious illness or injury incurred in the line of duty.

> **Note:** Spouses who work for the same employer are *jointly* entitled to a combined 12 weeks of leave in association with the birth of a child, placement of a child for adoption or foster care, and to care for a parent having serious health problems.

An FMLA leave can begin prior to the birth of a child, perhaps due to prenatal care issues or if the condition of the mother prevents her from working. The same leave situation can arise for an adoption, when a work absence is needed as part of the adoption process (such as a court appearance).

Leave can be taken intermittently, depending on the circumstances. For example, an employee may need to leave when it is medically necessary to care for a family member who is seriously ill. Employees should try to take these leaves in such a manner that they minimize the level of disruption caused for the employer's operations.

The FMLA restricts an FMLA leave of absence to those employees who:

- Have worked for the employer a total of at least 12 months, including a minimum of 1,250 hours in the last 12 months.
- Work at an employer facility where at least 50 of its employees work within a 75-mile radius.

EXAMPLE

Enrico Product Designs assists major corporations with their product designs, and so is located where client corporate headquarters are located – in New York, Chicago, and Los Angeles. The New York office employs 62 people, while the Chicago office employees 28 and the Los Angeles office employs 83. Melissa, an employee in the Chicago office, wants to go on leave in order to tend to her dying father, as does Bert, an employee in the New York office. Because none of the offices are within 75 miles of each other, the employees in the Chicago office

---

[8] A family member is classified as a spouse, child, and parents, though a parent in-law is not included.

(including Melissa) are not entitled to FMLA benefits. Conversely, Bert is entitled to FMLA benefits, since the office in which he is located has more than 50 employees.

EXAMPLE

Evan works for Eskimo Construction. He works in its Fairbanks office, which has 68 employees, and has worked there for the last five years. He asks for family leave, due to the birth of his baby son. In the preceding year, he worked 1,760 hours. Since he meets all FMLA criteria, he is fully covered by its provisions, and can take the requested leave.

Once an employer reaches the 50-employee threshold, it remains covered by the FMLA requirements until it reaches a point where it has not employed 50 personnel for 20 weeks in the current and preceding year.

Note: Some states have enacted laws that make the FMLA applicable to businesses having as few as 15 employees, and have expanded the definition of a family. One should verify the applicability of these state laws to the business.

If employees fall under the protection of the FMLA and take leaves of absence for the reasons allowed under the Act, continue to provide them with the medical insurance for which they had already signed up before going on leave. The employer can continue to require them to pay the same employee deduction that had been in effect prior to their leave of absence. If employees do not pay for their portion of the medical insurance within 30 days, the employer is entitled to cancel the insurance for the remaining period of their leave of absence. A few additional conditions of the FMLA are:

- If the medical coverage or the terms of the employee-paid portion of the insurance are altered during a person's leave of absence, these changes will apply to the person on leave.
- If employee medical insurance is cancelled due to non-payment, it must be restored once they return to work.
- Only continue a person's medical insurance through a period of leave. Other benefits are not addressed by the FMLA.

EXAMPLE

Jennifer Morris works for Suture Corporation. She takes a leave of absence to care for a terminally-ill child, which is covered under the FMLA. She had been covered under Suture's medical insurance plan prior to her leave of absence, under which she paid the company $300 per month as her portion of the expense.

While Ms. Morris is out on leave, the cost of Suture's medical insurance plan increases dramatically, causing the company to reduce benefits and increase the employee-paid portion of the cost to $500. Ms. Morris concludes that she cannot pay this increased amount, and stops paying Suture her share of the expense. Once her payment is 30 days overdue, Suture cancels her participation in the insurance plan.

Tip: Since the cost of providing medical coverage to an employee who is on leave can be quite high, consider adopting a formal review procedure and signed form that requires an employee to enumerate the reasons for going on leave, and the employer's evaluation of whether the leave falls under the FMLA. Also, provide the employee with specific instructions regarding when his or her share of medical insurance payments are to be paid to the employer, and the consequences of not making a timely payment.

FMLA Rights Posting

When an employer is covered by the FMLA, it is required to post a notice that is generally available to employees, noting employee rights and responsibilities under the Act. An employer can be fined if it is found to have willfully violated this requirement.

Leave Notice Rules

When employees want to take leave under the FMLA and where the need to do so is foreseeable, they must provide 30-day advance notice. When it is not foreseeable, employees should provide notice as soon as is practicable. In addition, the employer can mandate that medical certification of the underlying condition be provided, along with periodic recertifications. Further, employees should periodically notify the employer of their status, and whether they plan to return to work. Finally, an employer can require that employees who have been on FMLA leave obtain a certification that they are fit to return to work.

A notice of leave is considered to be valid even if the notice does not mention the FMLA. Employees merely need to request leave and provide a reason that qualifies under the FMLA.

Job Restoration Rules

A key requirement of the FMLA is that an employee must be given the same or equivalent job upon his or her return from leave, though no seniority accrues to an employee who is on leave.

Job restoration can be difficult for some positions, so the FMLA provides an exception. If an employee is salaried and paid in the top ten percent of employees, and restoring this person to his or her previous position would cause "substantial and grievous economic injury," this person's job is defined as a key position, and the employer may deny reinstatement to the individual. In order to deny job restoration under this exemption, the employer must notify an employee of his or her status as a key employee when the request for leave is made. In addition, the employer must notify the employee of the decision not to restore his or her job as soon as the decision is made, along with the reasons for doing so. Further, the employer must give the employee a reasonable opportunity to return to the workplace from the leave arrangement after this notice has been given. Finally, the employer must make a final determination about whether a person's job will be restored at the end of the leave period, if the person requests such restoration.

Federal Unemployment Tax Act (1939)

This Act originated the government-managed unemployment benefits system. Employers are required to pay a tax into the federal unemployment tax fund, which is used to fund state-level unemployment benefit programs. An employer is responsible for the payment of federal unemployment taxes (FUTA) if any of the following tests apply:

- *General test.* It paid wages of at least $1,500 in any calendar quarter in the current or preceding year, or had one or more employees for some portion of a day in at least 20 weeks in the current year or in at least 20 weeks in the preceding year. This test does not apply to farmworkers or household workers.
- *Farmworkers test.* It paid cash wages of at least $20,000 to farmworkers during any calendar quarter in the current or preceding year, or employed at least 10 farmworkers for some portion of a day in at least 20 weeks in the current year or in at least 20 weeks in the preceding year.
- *Household employees test.* It paid total cash wages of at least $1,000 to household employees in any calendar quarter in the current or preceding year. A household employee is an employee who performs household work in a private home, local college club, or local fraternity or sorority chapter.

The employer is responsible for FUTA taxes only for those employees falling into the preceding categories for which the employer is liable.

EXAMPLE

Aardvark Industries, maker of bulletproof upholstery, is only open for business when there are firm, prepaid orders for its very expensive upholstery products. Upon receipt of these orders, Aardvark farms out the work to a network of local stay-at-home parents who stitch together the materials and forward the completed goods back to the company for final assembly. Aardvark was founded in the immediately preceding year, when the owner worked for no wages for three months while he designed the product. In the fourth quarter, there was only one order, which required the payment of $1,200 in wages. Thus, Aardvark had no FUTA liability in that year.

In the next year, Aardvark receives an increasing stream of orders, resulting in it surpassing both the wage and time thresholds of the general FUTA test. Aardvark is liable for FUTA taxes in the next year.

Immigration Reform and Control Act (1986)

This Act bans an employer from knowingly hiring illegal aliens. It also requires a business to validate the immigration status of its employees. In addition, it bans employers from discriminating on the basis of United States citizenship. The Act is comprehensively applicable to entities of all sizes.

The employer must verify that every new employee is legally eligible to work in the United States. This verification involves having each employee complete Section 1 of the Form I-9, *Employment Eligibility Verification*, no later than the beginning of employment, which the employer must then verify. In the form, the employee presents appropriate types of identification, and the employer verifies these documents. The employer may also need to complete Section 3 of the form in cases where an employee's previous grant of work authorization has expired, and new evidence of work authorization is therefore required.

An example of the Form I-9 is shown on the next few pages, along with a listing of the types of documents that are considered acceptable evidence. In essence, an employee can present a single document that proves both identity and employment authorization (such as a U.S. passport or a permanent resident card), or two documents, one proving identity (such as a driver's license or voter registration card) and the other proving employment authorization (such as a social security card).

> **Tip:** Keep a photocopy of the employment eligibility documents submitted by all employees.

The employer does not file a completed Form I-9 with any government agency. Instead, it must retain these forms and make them available for inspection by U.S. government officials. The retention period is the longer of one year after a person's employment ends, or three years.

> **Tip:** If there are a large number of employees, it may be cost-effective to store completed I-9 forms in an electronic format, along with digital signatures. This format is allowed by law.

There are several ways in which an employer could discriminate on the basis of United States citizenship. For example, an employer could refuse to hire any job applicants who are not citizens or green card holders, or who are refugees whose employment authorizations have expiration dates.

If an employer is proven to have engaged in discriminatory practices, then it may be liable for back pay, as well as reinstatement of any employees who were discharged. There is also a discrimination penalty that increases in size, depending on the number of offenses committed by the employer.

Form I-9, Employment Eligibility Verification (page one)

Employment Eligibility Verification **Department of Homeland Security** U.S. Citizenship and Immigration Services		**USCIS** **Form I-9** OMB No.1615-0047 Expires 07/31/2026

START HERE: Employers must ensure the form instructions are available to employees when completing this form. Employers are liable for failing to comply with the requirements for completing this form. See below and the Instructions.

ANTI-DISCRIMINATION NOTICE: All employees can choose which acceptable documentation to present for Form I-9. Employers cannot ask employees for documentation to verify information in **Section 1**, or specify which acceptable documentation employees must present for **Section 2** or Supplement B, Reverification and Rehire. Treating employees differently based on their citizenship, immigration status, or national origin may be illegal.

Section 1. Employee Information and Attestation: Employees must complete and sign Section 1 of Form I-9 no later than the **first day of employment**, but not before accepting a job offer.

Last Name (Family Name)	First Name (Given Name)	Middle Initial (if any)	Other Last Names Used (if any)

Address (Street Number and Name)	Apt. Number (if any)	City or Town	State	ZIP Code

Date of Birth (mm/dd/yyyy)	U.S. Social Security Number	Employee's Email Address	Employee's Telephone Number

I am aware that federal law provides for imprisonment and/or fines for false statements, or the use of false documents, in connection with the completion of this form. I attest, under penalty of perjury, that this information, including my selection of the box attesting to my citizenship or immigration status, is true and correct.

Check one of the following boxes to attest to your citizenship or immigration status (See page 2 and 3 of the instructions.):

☐ 1. A citizen of the United States

☐ 2. A noncitizen national of the United States (See Instructions.)

☐ 3. A lawful permanent resident (Enter USCIS or A-Number.)

☐ 4. A noncitizen (other than Item Numbers 2. and 3. above) authorized to work until (exp. date, if any)

If you check **Item Number 4.**, enter one of these:

USCIS A-Number	OR	Form I-94 Admission Number	OR	Foreign Passport Number and Country of Issuance

Signature of Employee	Today's Date (mm/dd/yyyy)

If a preparer and/or translator assisted you in completing Section 1, that person MUST complete the Preparer and/or Translator Certification on Page 3.

Section 2. Employer Review and Verification: Employers or their authorized representative must complete and sign **Section 2** within three business days after the employee's first day of employment, and must physically examine, or examine consistent with an alternative procedure authorized by the Secretary of DHS, documentation from List A OR a combination of documentation from List B and List C. Enter any additional documentation in the Additional Information box; see Instructions.

	List A	OR	List B	AND	List C
Document Title 1					
Issuing Authority					
Document Number (if any)					
Expiration Date (if any)					
Document Title 2 (if any)		**Additional Information**			
Issuing Authority					
Document Number (if any)					
Expiration Date (if any)					
Document Title 3 (if any)					
Issuing Authority					
Document Number (if any)					
Expiration Date (if any)		☐ Check here if you used an alternative procedure authorized by DHS to examine documents.			

Certification: I attest, under penalty of perjury, that (1) I have examined the documentation presented by the above-named employee, (2) the above-listed documentation appears to be genuine and to relate to the employee named, and (3) to the best of my knowledge, the employee is authorized to work in the United States.	First Day of Employment (mm/dd/yyyy):

Last Name, First Name and Title of Employer or Authorized Representative	Signature of Employer or Authorized Representative	Today's Date (mm/dd/yyyy)

Employer's Business or Organization Name	Employer's Business or Organization Address, City or Town, State, ZIP Code

Form I-9, Employment Eligibility Verification (page two)

LISTS OF ACCEPTABLE DOCUMENTS

All documents containing an expiration date must be unexpired.
* Documents extended by the issuing authority are considered unexpired.
Employees may present one selection from List A or a
combination of one selection from List B and one selection from List C.
Examples of many of these documents appear in the Handbook for Employers (M-274).

LIST A		LIST B		LIST C
Documents that Establish Both Identity and Employment Authorization	**OR**	**Documents that Establish Identity**	**AND**	**Documents that Establish Employment Authorization**
1. U.S. Passport or U.S. Passport Card		1. Driver's license or ID card issued by a State or outlying possession of the United States provided it contains a photograph or information such as name, date of birth, gender, height, eye color, and address		1. A Social Security Account Number card, unless the card includes one of the following restrictions:
2. Permanent Resident Card or Alien Registration Receipt Card (Form I-551)				(1) NOT VALID FOR EMPLOYMENT
3. Foreign passport that contains a temporary I-551 stamp or temporary I-551 printed notation on a machine-readable immigrant visa		2. ID card issued by federal, state or local government agencies or entities, provided it contains a photograph or information such as name, date of birth, gender, height, eye color, and address		(2) VALID FOR WORK ONLY WITH INS AUTHORIZATION (3) VALID FOR WORK ONLY WITH DHS AUTHORIZATION
4. Employment Authorization Document that contains a photograph (Form I-766)		3. School ID card with a photograph		2. Certification of report of birth issued by the Department of State (Forms DS-1350, FS-545, FS-240)
5. For an individual temporarily authorized to work for a specific employer because of his or her status or parole:		4. Voter's registration card		3. Original or certified copy of birth certificate issued by a State, county, municipal authority, or territory of the United States bearing an official seal
a. Foreign passport; and		5. U.S. Military card or draft record		
b. Form I-94 or Form I-94A that has the following:		6. Military dependent's ID card		4. Native American tribal document
(1) The same name as the passport; and		7. U.S. Coast Guard Merchant Mariner Card		5. U.S. Citizen ID Card (Form I-197)
(2) An endorsement of the individual's status or parole as long as that period of endorsement has not yet expired and the proposed employment is not in conflict with any restrictions or limitations identified on the form.		8. Native American tribal document		6. Identification Card for Use of Resident Citizen in the United States (Form I-179)
		9. Driver's license issued by a Canadian government authority		7. Employment authorization document issued by the Department of Homeland Security
		For persons under age 18 who are unable to present a document listed above:		For examples, see **Section 7** and **Section 13** of the M-274 on **uscis.gov/i-9-central**.
6. Passport from the Federated States of Micronesia (FSM) or the Republic of the Marshall Islands (RMI) with Form I-94 or Form I-94A indicating nonimmigrant admission under the Compact of Free Association Between the United States and the FSM or RMI		10. School record or report card		The Form I-766, Employment Authorization Document, is a List A, **Item Number 4.** document, not a List C document.
		11. Clinic, doctor, or hospital record		
		12. Day-care or nursery school record		

Acceptable Receipts				
May be presented in lieu of a document listed above for a temporary period.				
For receipt validity dates, see the M-274.				
• Receipt for a replacement of a lost, stolen, or damaged List A document. • Form I-94 issued to a lawful permanent resident that contains an I-551 stamp and a photograph of the individual. • Form I-94 with "RE" notation or refugee stamp issued to a refugee.	**OR**	Receipt for a replacement of a lost, stolen, or damaged List B document.		Receipt for a replacement of a lost, stolen, or damaged List C document.

Form I-9, Employment Eligibility Verification (page three)

Supplement A,		**USCIS**
Preparer and/or Translator Certification for Section 1		**Form I-9**
Department of Homeland Security		**Supplement A**
U.S. Citizenship and Immigration Services		OMB No. 1615-0047
		Expires 07/31/2026

Last Name *(Family Name)* from **Section 1.**	First Name *(Given Name)* from **Section 1.**	Middle initial (if any) from **Section 1.**

Instructions: This supplement must be completed by any preparer and/or translator who assists an employee in completing Section 1 of Form I-9. The preparer and/or translator must enter the employee's name in the spaces provided above. Each preparer or translator must complete, sign, and date a separate certification area. Employers must retain completed supplement sheets with the employee's completed Form I-9.

I attest, under penalty of perjury, that I have assisted in the completion of Section 1 of this form and that to the best of my knowledge the information is true and correct.

Signature of Preparer or Translator		Date *(mm/dd/yyyy)*	
Last Name *(Family Name)*	First Name *(Given Name)*		Middle Initial *(if any)*
Address *(Street Number and Name)*	City or Town	State	ZIP Code

I attest, under penalty of perjury, that I have assisted in the completion of Section 1 of this form and that to the best of my knowledge the information is true and correct.

Signature of Preparer or Translator		Date *(mm/dd/yyyy)*	
Last Name *(Family Name)*	First Name *(Given Name)*		Middle Initial *(if any)*
Address *(Street Number and Name)*	City or Town	State	ZIP Code

I attest, under penalty of perjury, that I have assisted in the completion of Section 1 of this form and that to the best of my knowledge the information is true and correct.

Signature of Preparer or Translator		Date *(mm/dd/yyyy)*	
Last Name *(Family Name)*	First Name *(Given Name)*		Middle Initial *(if any)*
Address *(Street Number and Name)*	City or Town	State	ZIP Code

I attest, under penalty of perjury, that I have assisted in the completion of Section 1 of this form and that to the best of my knowledge the information is true and correct.

Signature of Preparer or Translator		Date *(mm/dd/yyyy)*	
Last Name *(Family Name)*	First Name *(Given Name)*		Middle Initial *(if any)*
Address *(Street Number and Name)*	City or Town	State	ZIP Code

Form I-9, Employment Eligibility Verification (page four)

Supplement B,		**USCIS**
Reverification and Rehire (formerly Section 3)		**Form I-9**
Department of Homeland Security		**Supplement B**
U.S. Citizenship and Immigration Services		OMB No. 1615-0047
		Expires 07/31/2026

Last Name *(Family Name)* from **Section 1.**	First Name *(Given Name)* from **Section 1.**	Middle initial (if any) from **Section 1.**

Instructions: This supplement replaces Section 3 on the previous version of Form I-9. Only use this page if your employee requires reverification, is rehired within three years of the date the original Form I-9 was completed, or provides proof of a legal name change. Enter the employee's name in the fields above. Use a new section for each reverification or rehire. Review the Form I-9 instructions before completing this page. Keep this page as part of the employee's Form I-9 record. Additional guidance can be found in the Handbook for Employers: Guidance for Completing Form I-9 (M-274)

Date of Rehire *(if applicable)*	New Name *(if applicable)*		
Date *(mm/dd/yyyy)*	Last Name (Family Name)	First Name (Given Name)	Middle Initial

Reverification: If the employee requires reverification, your employee can choose to present any acceptable List A or List C documentation to show continued employment authorization. Enter the document information in the spaces below.

Document Title	Document Number (if any)	Expiration Date (if any) (mm/dd/yyyy)

I attest, under penalty of perjury, that to the best of my knowledge, this employee is authorized to work in the United States, and if the employee presented documentation, the documentation I examined appears to be genuine and to relate to the individual who presented it.

Name of Employer or Authorized Representative	Signature of Employer or Authorized Representative	Today's Date *(mm/dd/yyyy)*

Additional Information (Initial and date each notation.)	☐ Check here if you used an alternative procedure authorized by DHS to examine documents.

Date of Rehire *(if applicable)*	New Name *(if applicable)*		
Date *(mm/dd/yyyy)*	Last Name (Family Name)	First Name (Given Name)	Middle Initial

Reverification: If the employee requires reverification, your employee can choose to present any acceptable List A or List C documentation to show continued employment authorization. Enter the document information in the spaces below.

Document Title	Document Number (if any)	Expiration Date (if any) (mm/dd/yyyy)

I attest, under penalty of perjury, that to the best of my knowledge, this employee is authorized to work in the United States, and if the employee presented documentation, the documentation I examined appears to be genuine and to relate to the individual who presented it.

Name of Employer or Authorized Representative	Signature of Employer or Authorized Representative	Today's Date *(mm/dd/yyyy)*

Additional Information (Initial and date each notation.)	☐ Check here if you used an alternative procedure authorized by DHS to examine documents.

Date of Rehire *(if applicable)*	New Name *(if applicable)*		
Date *(mm/dd/yyyy)*	Last Name (Family Name)	First Name (Given Name)	Middle Initial

Reverification: If the employee requires reverification, your employee can choose to present any acceptable List A or List C documentation to show continued employment authorization. Enter the document information in the spaces below.

Document Title	Document Number (if any)	Expiration Date (if any) (mm/dd/yyyy)

I attest, under penalty of perjury, that to the best of my knowledge, this employee is authorized to work in the United States, and if the employee presented documentation, the documentation I examined appears to be genuine and to relate to the individual who presented it.

Name of Employer or Authorized Representative	Signature of Employer or Authorized Representative	Today's Date *(mm/dd/yyyy)*

Additional Information (Initial and date each notation.)	☐ Check here if you used an alternative procedure authorized by DHS to examine documents.

Under the Act, an employer is not allowed to retaliate against an employee who files a complaint against it, or cooperates in an investigation of the organization.

Rehabilitation Act (1973)

An employer must be proactive in seeking out and employing individuals with disabilities. These activities must be documented in an affirmative action plan. The provisions of the Act are limited to federal government contractors and those entities receiving federal financial assistance. Within this classification, the Act applies to employers having at least 50 employees, and which have supply or service contracts with the federal government summing to at least $50,000.

Sarbanes-Oxley Act (2002)

Section 806 of the Sarbanes-Oxley Act protects corporate whistleblowers for providing information about securities fraud, shareholder fraud, bank fraud, mail fraud, wire fraud, or a violation of any Securities and Exchange Commission regulation. This protection is quite expansive; for example, an employee who reasonably believes that a securities violation is about to occur will be protected if the person reports the violation before it actually happens.

The whistleblower protection provision of the Act prohibits a broad range of retaliatory adverse employment actions, including discharging, demoting, suspending, threatening, harassing, or in any other manner discriminating against a whistleblower. Simply disclosing the identity of a whistleblower is considered actionable retaliation under the Act.

To prevail under the Sarbanes whistleblower provision, employees have to prove the following:

- That they engaged in a protected activity[9];
- That the employer knew that they were engaged in the protected activity;
- That they suffered an unfavorable personnel action as a result; and
- That the protected activity was a contributing factor in the unfavorable action.

Once an employee proves the elements of a Sarbanes whistleblower retaliation claim, the employer can avoid liability only if it proves by clear and convincing evidence that it would have taken the same unfavorable personnel action in the absence of the employee's protected behavior or conduct.

The Act does not provide for punitive damages, but does require all necessary relief to make the employee whole, which includes back pay and reinstatement.

Worker Adjustment and Retraining Notification Act (1988)

This Act (WARN) requires 60 calendar days' written notice when an employer plans to close a facility or conduct a mass layoff. The notice must be given to employees,

---

[9] A protected activity involves providing information about incorrect activities being undertaken by an employer, such as concealing material off-balance sheet transactions, underreporting corporate expenses, and circumventing internal controls.

the relevant state dislocated worker agency, the local chief elected official, and any union representing the employer's employees. The intent is to allow workers more time in which to prepare for the impending loss of their jobs. The provisions of WARN apply to situations where:

- The employer has at least 100 employees, not including anyone working less than 20 hours per week;
- A temporary or permanent facility closure will result in an employment loss for at least 50 full-time employees; or
- A mass layoff will result in employment loss for at least 500 full-time employees at an employment site, or for at least 50 full-time employees if they make up at least one-third of the active workforce.

The warning given must state whether the layoff will be temporary or permanent, the date of the expected layoff, and contact information for an employer official who can provide additional information.

Tip: Some states have more expansive laws on this topic. Check with the local state dislocated worker agency for the most up-to-date information on local laws.

There are exceptions to the WARN notification. It is not required when layoffs are associated with the end of a specific project where employees understood at the start of their employment that they would be hired for a limited period of time. A WARN notification is also not required when an employer conducts a layoff as a result of a strike.

EXAMPLE

ThreeDee Entertainment hires 500 graphic artists to provide the computer animation for the classic Accountants in Space trilogy. They are told at the start of their employment that they will be laid off once the trilogy has been completed, which is expected to be in three years. When the third film in the series is released to theaters three years later (to rapturous reviews), the artists are laid off. Given that they were told of their employment circumstances in advance, ThreeDee does not need to issue a WARN notification.

There are three other exceptions listed in the Act that allow a business to issue a notification on a reduced basis. In all of the following three cases, the employer must still provide as much notice as practicable, and state the reason for the reduced notification period:

- *Faltering company.* An employer is allowed to order a closing with less than 60-days' notice if it has a reasonable expectation that a full notice period would inhibit a deal that might otherwise keep the firm in business. This exception only applies when the organization has a realistic expectation of closing new business or obtaining fresh capital, but only by avoiding a public notice of a plant closure.

- *Unforeseen business circumstances.* A reduction in the notice requirement is allowed when there are business circumstances that the employer could not reasonably foresee at the point in time when notice would normally have been required. This typically involves a sudden and unexpected event that is outside of the control of the employer. A sudden downturn in the economy or the loss of a major customer might trigger this situation.
- *Natural disaster.* No notice is required at all when a natural disaster strikes a business. This exception only applies when there is a direct relationship between a natural disaster and a layoff. For example, a tsunami wipes out a company's production facility that is located on a coastline.

When an employer does not comply with the terms of this Act, it can be liable for back pay, benefits, and any medical costs that otherwise would have been covered if employees had remained employed during the notice period. There are no provisions in the Act for punitive damages.

Occupational Safety and Health Act (1970)

The Occupational Safety and Health Act is a federal law that is intended to improve the level of worker and workplace safety, and applies to those organizations engaged in interstate commerce. The Act does so by mandating the elimination of employee exposure to toxic chemicals, dangerous equipment, excessively high noise levels, unsanitary conditions, and excessive amounts of high or low temperature stress. Generally, the Act mandates that an employer must maintain a place of employment that is free of any hazards that might cause death or serious harm to employees.

The Act also created the Occupational Safety and Health Administration (OSHA), which is part of the Department of Labor. OSHA's role is to set and enforce workplace health and safety standards. OSHA is authorized to inspect and investigate any workplace covered by the Act. OSHA prioritizes inspections as follows (in declining order of importance):

1. *Imminent danger.* These inspections are targeted at conditions that pose a reasonable certainty of immediate death or physical harm.
2. *Catastrophes and fatal accidents.* These are investigations of deaths or accidents that hospitalized three or more employees.
3. *Complaints and referrals.* These are investigations of employee complaints about workplace hazards.
4. *Programmed inspections.* These inspections are based on a determination that special hazards exist within an industry or specific workplace.

Whenever an inspection reveals a violation, OSHA issues a citation that sets a time period within which the employer must remediate the issue found. When an inspection uncovers an imminent danger, a restraining order may be imposed that forces the employer to immediately remediate the problem or move employees from the impacted location.

When a penalty is levied on an employer, the amount is based on the size of the business, the gravity of the violation, the employer's good faith, and the employer's history of previous violations.

OSHA operates a voluntary protection program (VPP), which recognizes employers that have implemented effective safety and health management systems and maintain injury and illness rates below National Bureau of Labor Statistics averages for their respective industries. An operational VPP requires management, labor, and an OSHA representative to work together to prevent fatalities, injuries, and illnesses through a system that focuses on hazard prevention and control, worksite analysis, and training. To participate, employers must submit an application to OSHA and undergo an onsite evaluation by a team of safety and health professionals. Union support is required for applicants represented by a bargaining unit. Program participants are re-evaluated every three to five years to remain in the program. Participants in the program are exempt from OSHA inspections for as long as they maintain their VPP status.

OSHA requires the use of material safety data sheets (MSDS), which are detailed technical bulletins that must be posted for general reading by employees. An MSDS is intended to make employees aware of chemical hazards and how to avoid them. Further, OSHA requires employers to itemize all job-related injuries and illnesses requiring medical treatment on the OSHA Form 300.

An employer can seek a temporary variance from OSHA that exempts it from one of the agency's rules. A variance may be granted when the employer is unable to comply with a standard as of its effective date, due to a shortage of skilled workers, materials, or facilities. In this case, the employer is committing to protect employees from the targeted hazard, and it will comply with the standard as soon as practicable. A granted variance will expire after no more than two years.

It is also possible for an employer to obtain a permanent variance from an OSHA rule. This may be granted when the employer has implemented an alternative method that ensures the same level of workplace safety as the applicable rule.

Any claims against an employer that breach the mandate to maintain a hazard-free workplace must prove that the employer failed to furnish a workplace free of hazard, that its employees were exposed to that hazard, that the hazard was recognized, that the hazard was likely to cause death or serious injury, and that a feasible method exists to correct the hazard.

EXAMPLE

Choppy Cruises operates a ferry that crosses an especially rough area of open water. Despite numerous complaints by the crew, the ferry owner has not installed a protective railing around the stern of the ferry, where crew members need to congregate during the docking procedure. This is a potential OSHA violation, since there is a feasible method to correct it (installing a railing).

> **Note:** Employees may resist some OSHA rules, such as the mandate to wear a hard hat in certain situations. In these cases, the employer is still responsible for enforcing the rule.

An employer can challenge a standard before OSHA enforces it. Or, if an employer waits to be cited by OSHA for not following a standard, then it has 15 working days in which to contest the citation. Hearings for contested citations are before an administrative law judge.

The Act contains a prohibition against retaliation. This means that an employer cannot discharge or discriminate against an employee who files a complaint or exercises any other rights under the Act. This includes situations in which an employee refuses work due to a reasonable fear of death or serious injury. The available forms of relief include backpay, compensatory damages, and reinstatement.

Employers must maintain records relating to workplace safety, noting instances of non-minor workplace injuries and illnesses, plus any exposures to toxic or harmful materials.

OSHA applies to most private employers, though employers with 10 or fewer employees and good safety records are exempt from regular inspections. It does not apply to public employers, though federal agencies must maintain safety and health programs that are consistent with the Act.

Summary

The major laws noted in this chapter are by no means all of the laws that can impact labor relations. There are many state and local laws that expand upon the provisions of these federal laws, either to make them applicable to more employers, add more requirements, or expand upon penalties.

When does a law apply to an employer's specific circumstances? The triggering issue may be the number of employees working for it. However, the employee count depends upon how an "employee" is defined, especially if there are a number of part-time employees working for the employer. Given the variable applicability of certain laws, it makes sense to go over the laws in this chapter at least once a year (if not more frequently) to see if any laws now apply that did not in the past.

The most important advice when dealing with labor law is to retain the services of a competent attorney. Have this person go over the employer's general labor situation when first retained to see if there are any legal violations occurring, and correct anything found. Also, seek out the attorney's advice whenever there is a labor issue that appears to infringe upon a law. In short, do not try to muddle through without an expert on labor law – doing so can result in a serious legal violation that will require expensive remediation.

Chapter 3
Additional Employment Concepts

Introduction

In this chapter, we will expand upon a number of the concepts introduced in the preceding chapter, including categories of employment discrimination, bona fide occupational qualifications, affirmative action, applicant testing, and much more. These topics all relate to the legal rights of workers and how an employer should deal with them. But first, we will point out the practical benefits of providing equal employment opportunities to all employees.

Equal Employment Opportunity

Equal employment opportunity (EEO) is the concept of not discriminating against an employee or candidate for a position based on their race, color, religion, national origin, sex, physical or mental disability, or age. A business that does not employ EEO principles is engaged in discrimination.

The concept of EEO is not just something that is mandated under the law; it is also good practice. When an employer surveys the complete range of possible candidates for a position or a promotion opportunity, it is maximizing the probability of improving the quality of its workforce. Here are several examples:

- *Older employees.* An older employee is more likely to be mature and have greater experience. Accordingly, an older person is more likely to be an efficient worker, and may be a better manager.
- *Female employees.* Many highly educated women have left the workforce to raise children, and now want to return to the workforce. If some accommodation can be made to give them flexible working hours, an employer can benefit massively from their high levels of training.
- *Physical disability.* Physically disabled people can likely still function just fine in the workforce, as long as some accommodation is made to work around their disabilities, perhaps through job redesign or some physical modifications to the workplace.

In short, a business that discriminates is not maximizing its use of the available workforce.

The Protected Class Concept

The protected class concept is a term used in anti-discrimination law to define a characteristic of a person that cannot be targeted for discrimination. The following table presents all protected classes, as defined through various legislative enactments and court cases.

Protected Classes

Age (over 40)	Family status	Religion
Citizenship	Genetic information	Sex
Color	National origin	Sexual orientation
Disability status	Pregnancy	Veteran status
	Race	

The most basic description of the national origin protected class is that it applies to those individuals who came from, or whose ancestors came from, another country. However, ongoing court interpretations of the concept have expanded over the years, so that the national origin concept is now one of the more broad-based classes. All of the following concepts are now considered to be contained within the national origin class:

- Attendance at a school or place of worship used by people of a national group
- Being married to someone in a national group
- Being associated with someone in a national group
- Membership in an organization that promotes the interests of a national group
- Association with an organization that promotes the interests of a national group
- Use of a person's name that is associated with a national group

Such a broad interpretation means that an employer must be especially careful to create a workplace where there are no ethnic slurs or other types of conduct related to national origin.

Categories of Employment Discrimination

There are two types of employment discrimination, which are disparate treatment and adverse impact. *Disparate treatment* is the most basic form of employment discrimination, and refers to the varying treatment of employees based on their age, color, national origin, race, religion, or sex. An example of disparate treatment is testing the reading ability of women, but not men. *Adverse impact* is the use of apparently neutral selection procedures that have the effect of excluding a disproportionate number of employees based on their age, color, national origin, race, religion, or sex, and where the selection procedures are not job-related. For example, a warehousing operation may require that a candidate be able to lift a heavy weight, which would likely exclude from consideration a larger proportion of women than men. If the warehouse jobs are all related to operating forklifts, there is no actual need to lift heavy inventory items. In this case, the job requirement is discriminatory against women.

Tip: If a selection procedure could be considered discriminatory, search for a replacement procedure that can predict job performance, but which does not exclude a disproportionate number of a protected class.

A selection procedure is considered to have an adverse impact if, as a result of its use, a protected group is not hired at a rate of at least eighty percent of that group of individuals achieving the best result under the selection procedure. This is sometimes referred to as the four-fifths rule. The formula used to calculate adverse impact is as follows:

$$\frac{\text{Success rate of lowest-achieving applicant group}}{\text{Success rate of highest-achieving applicant group}} = \text{Proportion of adverse impact}$$

The groups that the EEOC has designated for measurement under this formula are:

- Asians
- Blacks
- Hispanics
- Men
- Native Americans
- Women

EXAMPLE

The human resources director of Mole Industries is calculating whether there has been any adverse impact resulting from the company's hiring practices in the production area in the past year. During that time, the company hired 250 employees. Of that group, 160 of the hires were men and 90 were women. The qualified applicant pool during the past year was 500 men and 400 women. The success rate of the men was therefore 32% (calculated as 160 hires divided by 500 applicants). The success of the women was 23% (calculated as 90 hires divided by 400 applicants).

The director plugs this information into the adverse impact formula to derive the following result:

$$\frac{23\% \text{ Women success rate}}{32\% \text{ Men success rate}} = 72\% \text{ Proportion of adverse impact}$$

Since the outcome is less than eighty percent, adverse impact exists.

Adverse impact requires constant monitoring. The human resources staff should routinely calculate adverse impact, and notify management if the calculation drops below the eighty percent level. In addition, be certain that only the most qualified applicants are recruited, since this group is included in the applicant pool on which the calculation is based.

A selection procedure may result in a clear case of adverse impact. If so, an employer has a choice of either finding a different approach to selection, or of validating that the procedure has a high correlation with improved job performance. If validation of the procedure can be proven, the employer must also prove that it would incur prohibitive training expenses if it did not use this procedure. If such is the case, the employer can continue to use the selection procedure because there is an established business necessity.

Bona Fide Occupational Qualifications

A bona fide occupational qualification (BFOQ) is a situation in which the sex, religion, or national origin of a person is a valid reason for employing him or her. For example, a model for women's clothes needs to be a woman. Similarly, a religious institution operating a school may require that all teachers hired into that school have the same religious beliefs advocated by the parent institution. Or, an employer engaged in cross-border sales to Mexico requires that all of its sales staff speak Spanish.

As just demonstrated, there are valid instances where the BFOQ concept applies. However, it is not intended to be applied across a large number of situations as a general excuse for discrimination.

Affirmative Action

If an employer is a contractor of the federal government, it must comply with affirmative action rules. The affirmative action concept states that an employer must be proactive in ensuring the employment and subsequent treatment of individuals without regard to their race, religion, color, sex, or national origin. Affirmative action applies to the following areas:

- Recruiting
- Hiring
- Promotions and demotions
- Job transfers
- Selection for training programs
- Compensation
- Layoffs and terminations

An employer impacted by affirmative action must post information about the program in the workplace. In addition, there must be a detailed policy statement supporting affirmative action.

An affirmative action program is designed to create a workforce that is proportional to its representation in the relevant labor market of the business. To do so, the distribution of the current workforce is compared to the relevant labor market and any disparities are noted. The employer then creates annual and ultimate goals that are reasonably attainable to increase the hiring and subsequent treatment of minorities and women in order to reduce these disparities. In more detail, the following steps are included in an affirmative action plan:

1. Assign responsibility for the program to a person having access to senior management.
2. Create groups of jobs, aggregated by similar duties and responsibilities.
3. Classify current employees by job group.
4. Calculate the percentages of minorities and women currently in each job group.
5. Obtain demographic information on the available labor pool for each job group.
6. Compare the proportions of protected classes in each job group to the related labor pool.
7. Set goals to improve the representation of those protected classes that are currently under-represented in the workforce.
8. Periodically review with management the results of the program, including actions taken to achieve designated goals.

EXAMPLE

The human resources manager of Oberlin Acoustics is reviewing the company's affirmative action plan. She notes that the availability of women for the clerical job group is 40%, but that the employment of women in that job group is only 20%. Accordingly, she sets a goal to double female employment in this job group.

There are a number of steps that can be taken to increase the representation of minorities and women in an employer's workforce. Consider the following options:

- Contact organizations that can refer minority and female job applicants to the employer
- Contact current minority and women employees, and ask them to refer candidates
- Recruit at schools whose attendees are primarily minorities or women
- Engage in job fairs in the relevant labor markets
- Create special employment programs targeted at minorities and women

A government contractor may be investigated by the Office of Federal Contract Compliance Programs (OFCCP) to see if it is in compliance with affirmative action. This investigation may be triggered by the past affirmative action performance of a contractor, complaints received, employment changes that may result from a contract that is about to be awarded, and similar issues. If an employer is not in compliance, the OFCCP will first attempt to persuade the employer to take compliance steps. If this fails, a formal notice is issued, along with a request for a response. The parties then enter into a written contract to bring the business into compliance. If violations are not corrected, an employer can be passed over for future contract awards by the government, and current contracts may be suspended or terminated.

Interviewing Issues

An employer can be sued on the outcome of a hiring decision if the interviewer asked a candidate about a variety of topics, such as a person's family plans, religion, age, national origin, or gender. It is not especially difficult to warn interviewers away from these topics. It can be substantially *more* difficult for an interviewer to steer clear of these topics when the candidate brings them up. This situation may arise when the interviewer asks an open-ended "essay style" question, and the candidate diverges off topic into one of these discriminatory areas. One option is for the interviewer to immediately take charge of the discussion and bring it back to issues pertaining solely to the job. Another alternative is to state up front that the hiring decision will be based solely on a person's job qualifications, and that the other topics should not be addressed.

There are a number of topics that should be avoided during an interview, since they might give the impression that the interviewer is engaging in discriminatory behavior. The following exhibit contains examples of questions to be avoided, grouped by protected class.

Examples of Discriminatory Questions

Protected Class	Discriminatory Questions
Age	Asking for high school or college graduation dates
Family status	Asking for a female applicant's maiden name
	Asking whether a female applicant wants to be addressed as "Miss" or "Mrs."
Religion	Asking what holidays a person observes
Veteran status	Asking about the type of discharge received from the military

One area in which it *is* permissible to ask a candidate's age is when a person appears to be so young that the employer might be in danger of violating a child labor law. In this case, it is permissible to ask if the person is under the age of 18.

The application process should only include questions that are asked to *all* applicants. This means that questions addressed only to a protected class are considered discriminatory. For example, an employer might ask a female candidate if she has children, but not male candidates. This line of questioning can easily be construed to mean that the employer intends to deny employment to the female candidate on the assumption that she needs time away from work to raise her children, but would not accord the same treatment to a male candidate.

Applicant Testing

An employer may find that it can select higher-quality candidates by first screening them with a variety of tests. If so, be aware that these tests may be unintentionally discriminatory against a protected class. This situation arises when there is a significant rate of exclusion when a particular test is applied to candidates. When this is the case, avoid using the test, unless it can be proven that the test is necessary for the specific position for which the employer is recruiting.

EXAMPLE

The Sliced Hog Meat Processing Company requires that everyone applying for a job of any kind must have a high school diploma. A black candidate who does not have a high school diploma brings a discrimination lawsuit against the company. Sliced Hog loses the resulting trial when it is proven that a diploma is not really necessary in order to engage in meatpacking work, and that a higher percentage of blacks than whites in the local labor market have not obtained a high school diploma. Thus, the diploma requirement is discriminatory against a protected class.

> **Tip:** Continue to review the appropriateness of tests to screen for specific jobs, since the nature of the jobs may change over time.

Medical Examinations

It is legitimate for an employer to require a candidate to undergo a medical examination, but only if the examination is directly related to the requirements of the position for which the person is being considered. Thus, a delivery person who is expected to lift heavy boxes should be required to undergo a medical examination, while there may be no valid reason for requiring a clerk to do so.

A medical examination can only be required *after* a candidate has been offered a job. This offer can be contingent upon the person passing the examination. The specific intent of the examination is to determine whether a candidate is physically capable of performing the tasks listed in a job description. If the result of an examination indicates that a candidate's performance would be adversely impacted by his physical condition, the employer can rescind its job offer.

Drug Tests

An employer may elect to discharge any employee who refuses to take a drug test. The employer would be justified in doing so as long as the test was needed to ensure that employees did not put themselves or others in danger (such as workers on an oil rig), the test was to be conducted within normal employee working hours, and employees were notified of the test. In short, an employer can shrug off most challenges to drug testing, as long as it follows a standard procedure for notifying employees and making it reasonably convenient for them. However, this will vary, depending on state law.

Genetic Tests

Tests are now available that can scan the genetic structure of employees to see if they are predisposed to various inherited diseases or cancers. An employer could potentially use this information to deny employment to a job candidate, on the grounds that the individual is more likely to become ill, thereby costing the employer lost productivity and increased medical costs. Given this concern, the EEOC has stated that a person having a genetic predisposition to a disease is covered by the Americans with Disabilities Act. In addition, the Genetic Information Nondiscrimination Act mandates that genetic information cannot be improperly used in making employment decisions related to hiring and firing, placements in certain positions, or in regard to promotion opportunities.

Polygraph Tests

A polygraph test employs stress testing to detect when a person is telling a lie. Such a test could be used to confirm the information that a candidate states in a resume. The Employee Polygraph Protection Act (EPPA) rendered this testing method illegal for most private employers, except for the following situations:

- An employer is engaged in security services
- An employer is engaged in the production or distribution of pharmaceuticals
- There is a reasonable suspicion that an employee has engaged in an illegal activity in the workplace

Polygraph testing is still legal when applied to government employees, and is actively used for those individuals handling secret government information.

If a person is subjected to a polygraph test, she has the following rights under the EPPA:

- Must be notified of the test in advance and in writing
- Can refuse to take such a test, as well as discontinue a test in progress
- Can refuse to have the results of such a test disclosed to an unauthorized individual

A business could use an honest test instead of a polygraph test, which poses a number of questions to a job applicant in order to discern whether the person is emotionally stable, dependable, and so forth. However, the questions must be structured to avoid violating their rights, such as by posing questions about their sexual orientation or religious preferences. An employer may elect to administer such tests in order to root out any job applicants that could potentially harm customers or fellow employees.

Credit Checks

An employer may run a credit check on job applicants, with the intent of weeding out those applicants with low credit scores. However, if the use of credit checks results in a disproportionate number of people from a protected group being rejected from consideration for employment, this could be considered discrimination. A better approach is to tie credit checks to specific positions, such as those dealing with employer funds. Thus, the use of a credit check can be traced back to the need for integrity in a cashier, but it would be more difficult to make the same argument for an engineering position.

Summary

Generally, an employer is more likely to make use of any testing available to evaluate job applicants that are to be placed in positions where they will interact with third parties, such as customers or suppliers. They do not want to be found negligent in the evaluation of applicants who might cause harm to others.

Ex-Offender Hiring

A large number of organizations have a standard practice of never hiring ex-offenders. There can be a good reason for this, such as keeping sex offenders out of day care facilities. But in many other cases, there is no immediate reason why an ex-offender cannot be hired. Employers simply turn down their applications as standard practice, sometimes even asking on applications if an applicant has ever been convicted of a crime.

Ex-offenders are not a protected class under federal law, but there may be laws at the state or local level that bar employers from asking about criminal convictions on the job application. Doing so at least allows a candidate the opportunity to interview for a position; if an employer is sufficiently impressed, a subsequent background check may be ignored in order to give the candidate a chance.

To be safe, an employer should check with a labor law attorney to see if the criminal conviction question should be removed from its standard job application form.

The Employee Manual

Many organizations issue an employee manual to newly-hired employees. This document codifies the human resources policies of an organization, as well as a number of procedures and rules, and also describes the benefit plan. It is a useful basis for the consistent treatment of employees, which can reduce the risk of being targeted by discrimination lawsuits. It is also useful for informing employees about the process for reporting issues to management, such as sexual harassment complaints. Finally, an employee manual makes a business appear to deal fairly with its employees, which can enhance morale.

Typical contents of an employee manual include the following:

- Welcome letter
- Employer background information
- Key employer policies, such as:
    - Equal employment opportunity

- o Sexual harassment
- o Internet access
- o Vacation

- Essential employer rules, such as
  - o Attendance
  - o Dress code
  - o Holidays
  - o Paid and unpaid absences
  - o Pay dates
  - o Standards of conduct and disciplinary rules
  - o Timekeeping
  - o Work hours

- Safety issues, such as fire exit maps and safety guidelines
- Employee benefits

There are some legal issues to be observed when constructing an employee manual. In particular, have a labor law attorney review it to ensure that there are no statements in the manual that could get the employer in trouble if an employee were later to take issue with it. Also, verify that the employer's actual labor practices mirror what is stated in the manual – again, so that there can be no justifiable cause for employee complaints.

An employee manual could be construed as a contract, which could be used by a fired employee as the basis for a wrongful termination lawsuit. To avoid this, the employer should include a prominently-displayed and clearly-written disclaimer in the employee manual, noting that employment is at-will, that the manual is not a contract, and that the employer has the right to modify the terms of the manual. Otherwise, if the manual were to be construed as a contract, then any changes to it without employee acceptance of the changes, and in exchange for some form of consideration, could be considered non-binding on the employees.

Tip: List the beginning and ending dates and times for the organization's work week in the employee manual, so that everyone knows the time period over which they are being paid.

The English-Only Rule

When an employer has a multi-lingual workforce and requires that employees speak English, this is not necessarily considered discriminatory behavior. In many instances, it is a business necessity for employees to communicate in English as part of their jobs. For example, speaking English may be necessary when there is a safety alert in the workplace, and it is essential that all employees understand the evacuation instructions being given to them. Similarly, it may be necessary to speak English on a production line, in order to incorporate feedback into the production process to avoid manufacturing flaws. Or, a team working on a project needs to speak English in order to complete their assigned work.

To reduce the risk of a discrimination charge based on an English-only rule, an employer can allow employees to speak in their native languages during break periods. Also, if the English-only rule is applied, do so universally to all employees; targeting only those employees speaking a certain language would likely be considered discriminatory.

EXAMPLE

Syrup By Design converts maple syrup into a variety of products, including maple-infused bacon and maple ice cream. To access the best maple syrup, it is located in northern New Hampshire, near the Quebec border. There are many French-speaking workers who live in this area. The company has a policy that requires all employees to speak English while on the company premises, including during breaks. When management spots a French-speaker who violates this policy, it replaces the person with an English-speaking worker. Gerard, who speaks French, files a charge with the EEOC that the company's English-only policy discriminates against him due to his national origin.

The EEOC investigator finds that English proficiency is not needed for any of the positions currently held by French-speaking workers, indicating that the policy violates the law.

Sexual Harassment

Sexual harassment arises when a person in a position of power creates a hostile work environment or attempts to extort sexual favors from other employees. It also violates Title VII of the Civil Rights Act. The EEOC defines sexual harassment as including the following:

- *Condition of employment.* The affected employee must submit to this conduct as a condition of employment.
- *Employment decisions.* How the affected employee responds to (accepts or rejects) this conduct is used to make employment decisions (such as granting promotions).
- *Work environment.* The result of this conduct is an offensive work environment. Examples of such an environment are a pattern of threatening behavior, intimidation, sexual stereotyping, and the display of graphic materials. A hostile work environment is considered to be present when discriminatory conduct is frequent and severe, interferes with one's work performance, and is physically threatening or humiliating.
- *Work performance.* The result of this conduct can interfere with a person's job performance.

When assessing whether a hostile work environment exists, one should consider the totality of the circumstances, whether a reasonable person would find the situation to be hostile or abusive, and whether the person making the charge perceives the conduct to be unwelcome. Normally, a series of harassment incidents would be needed to prove that a hostile work environment exists; however, a hostile environment is presumed to exist after a small number of severe cases of harassment.

EXAMPLE

Anna is the only female employee in a tractor supply company that employs 40 people. After one year of work, she is promoted to a sales position. Following this advancement, the fulfillment manager and repairs manager stop by to discuss how she will interact with their departments. During the conversation, they note that a "pretty face" is needed to bring in more sales, and that she may have to sleep with a few customers to bring in sales.

Both managers continue to make similar comments in front of Anna's co-workers over the following months, continually suggesting that she is only bringing in sales because she is accommodating the sexual demands of her customers. Eventually, Anna complains to the company owner, who does nothing. She then files a charge with the EEOC. The investigator assigned to the case notes that a reasonable person in Anna's position would find these comments to be hostile and offensive.

> **Note:** The victim of sexual harassment does not need to be of the opposite sex, and can be a man or a woman.

An employer can also be held liable when its employees are subjected to harassment by a supplier or customer, and it takes no corrective action.

EXAMPLE

Abby is a senior architect with Burton & Howard, a mid-sized national architectural consulting firm. She is assigned to be the lead architect on a major project involving the design of a new headquarters building. In this role, she must interact with the client's president on a daily basis.

The client makes numerous comments about her looks, assigns her to an office next to his, and repeatedly demands that she go on trips with him on weekends to view comparable buildings that he would like to emulate in the new headquarters building. During a recent lunch, he touches her inappropriately under the table.

The next day, Abby meets with Mike Burton, one of the firm's owners, and requests that she be pulled off the engagement. The company needs the fees from this project, so Mike advises her to remain on the project until its completion. Because Burton & Howard did not take remedial action, it could be subject to a sexual harassment claim.

Further, it is unlawful to retaliate against anyone who complains about employment practices that discriminate based on sex, or who participates in a complaint against the employer.

An employer is liable for any sexual harassment activity engaged in by one of its supervisors, even if there was no knowledge by management of any harassment activity. However, the employer can mitigate this liability by creating and maintaining a system to prevent and correct any instances of harassment. If a supervisor engages in an activity that results in a tangible employment action[10], then the employer is always liable, and there is no way to mitigate this liability. Thus, if a supervisor transfers a female employee into an undesirable posting from which there is little chance of promotion because she refused his advances, this would be considered a tangible employment action.

To limit the liability of the employer from sexual harassment claims, the following actions should be taken and routinely reinforced:

- *Policy*. Create a detailed policy that clearly defines sexual harassment, describes the complaint steps to follow, and states that the employer will take immediate corrective action. Also note that anyone claiming such harassment will be protected from retaliation. The policy should be written so that it is easily understandable by all employees. In addition, it should be posted in central locations and in the employee manual.
- *Process*. Create a clear process by which sexual harassment claims are initiated and dealt with. The employer should deal with these claims promptly and firmly; taking minimal corrective steps can be viewed as condoning sexual harassment. Also, the presence of a clear process for dealing with sexual harassment becomes part of the workplace environment, and so is considered to be a mitigation of a hostile work environment.

Tip: Set up an anonymous phone number through which complaints can be reported to an impartial person. Also, set up an alternative contact person, in case the main contact is the person harassing employees.

- *Discipline*. The level of discipline imposed on a harasser should be in proportion to the level of offense. Thus, a minor one-time offense may result in a mandatory training class, while a pattern of severe offenses is more likely result in one's discharge. Any action that does not alter a harasser's compensation, benefits, duties, or position should not be considered discipline.

Note: Examples of disciplinary outcomes include (in ascending order of severity) counseling, a warning, transfer, demotion, suspension from work, and discharge.

- *Training*. Conduct periodic training regarding sexual harassment, with particular emphasis on the employer's policy and claims process.

---

[10] A tangible employment action is a significant change in a worker's employment status. Examples include hiring, firing, promotion, demotion, undesirable reassignment, a decision causing a significant change in benefits, and compensation decisions.

- *Posters.* Reinforce the preceding points with posters displayed in the workplace, explaining the employer's sexual harassment policy and process.

Management should take action as soon as it is informed of a sexual harassment claim. As an immediate step, it should consider transferring the person who is alleged to have engaged in harassment, or altering the person's work schedule so that there is no interaction between the accuser and the accused. The person lodging the complaint should not be transferred, because this could be construed as unlawful retaliation. Further, the alleged harasser should not be the supervisor of the person who conducts the investigation.

When conducting an investigation of a sexual harassment claim, the investigator will typically have to search for corroborating evidence, since the interactions between the two parties may have been behind a closed door. Corroborating evidence includes talking to other people who observed or talked to the claimant immediately after the alleged event to see if there were any changes in his or her behavior. In addition, the investigator could determine whether other people were subjected to similar behavior by the alleged harasser.

EXAMPLE

Christine charges that her boss inappropriately touched her during a series of performance review meetings, and stated that he would give her a raise if she engaged in certain sexual acts with him. There are no witnesses, and the supervisor categorically denies her allegations.

The investigator interviews other people in the office, and finds that Christine talked to four of her co-workers immediately after these review meetings, and looked distraught at the time. In addition, she complained to the company owner immediately after each of the meetings.

Based on the corroborating testimony and her ongoing complaints to management, Christine has solid backing for her sexual harassment claim.

> **Tip:** Establish an annual date on which the sexual harassment policy and process are re-distributed to employees, to reinforce the employer's position on this topic.

In addition, have a documentation system in place for recording the information associated with all sexual harassment claims. This should include the recordation of detailed statements from the accuser and accused. Having this information gives the organization a firm basis upon which to make decisions, and also protects it in case of a lawsuit.

An offshoot of sexual harassment is pregnancy discrimination. As the name implies, this is discriminatory behavior that is based on a woman's pregnancy or related medical issues. An employer cannot refuse to hire a woman because of her pregnancy. If a person is unable to perform assigned tasks due to pregnancy, then the employer must treat her the same as any other temporarily-disabled employee. Thus, if an employer generally allows any temporarily-disabled employee to take sick time, then it must extend the same privilege to a pregnant employee. This also means that an employer must hold a job open for an employee's pregnancy-related absence for just as long as it would do so for any employee who is temporarily disabled for other reasons.

> **Note:** Discrimination against an employee because that person is transgender is considered by the EEOC to be discriminatory behavior due to sex, which is prohibited by the Civil Rights Act.

Intentional Infliction of Emotional Distress

A charge of intentional infliction of emotional distress (IIED) allows a person to recover for severe emotional distress caused by another person who intentionally or recklessly inflicts emotional distress by behaving in an extreme and outrageous way. An employee can recover damages for emotional distress suffered when an employer acts wrongfully, such as by discriminating against the person on the basis of race. This charge can also apply in cases where the conduct of the employer is otherwise considered to be lawful. For example, an employee could successfully bring a charge of IIED after being legally discharged from work, but where the employer did so in an impermissible manner. For example, parading a fired employee out the door and throwing his belongings into the parking lot is probably not a good idea.

A case of IIED can be proven when an employee can justify that the employer's conduct was extreme and outrageous; beyond the limits of all human decency; the employer intended to and did cause severe emotional distress; and the resulting distress was so severe that no reasonable person could be expected to endure it.

Invasion of Employee Privacy

Whether an employer invades the privacy of an employee in the workplace depends on that person's reasonable expectation of privacy in the workplace. This determination depends on when an employer's conduct would be considered highly offensive to a reasonable person.

EXAMPLE

Martha works at a restaurant, where she is given a personal locker. She puts a personal lock on it, and stores various personal belongings in it. Later, the restaurant manager suspects that food is being stolen, so he cuts off the lock and rummages through her locker.

A court would likely find that this was an invasion of employee privacy, because the restaurant had allowed her to put a lock on the locker, thereby giving her a reasonable expectation of privacy.

In the preceding example, the employee's expectations for privacy would be lowered if the employer had mandated that no locks be used, or by stating in the employee manual that management could search the employee lockers at any time.

The invasion of employee privacy concept can be applied elsewhere in the workplace. For example, an invasion of privacy could be claimed for an employee's computer files, emails, and phone calls. An employer can combat the invasion of privacy issue by stating in the employee manual that all of these items may be monitored by the employer. Doing so reduces employee expectations of privacy, which in turn reduces the employer's potential liability.

According to the Wiretap Act, an employer generally must obtain the consent of one or both of the parties to a communication before it is allowable to listen in on a phone call or view employee emails. Just because an employee has left an email password lying on his desk does not imply that the person has given his consent for the employer to use this information to access email accounts set up with a third-party provider.

Retaliation

When a job candidate or employee files a discrimination claim, it is illegal for an employer to retaliate against that person. This means that the employer cannot harass, fire, demote, or refuse to promote someone in retaliation for a discrimination charge or participating in a discrimination hearing, or otherwise opposing the concept of discrimination. Retaliation can also be considered to apply to someone who is a close associate of such an employee.

EXAMPLE

An employee files a charge with the EEOC that her employer discriminated against her based on a disability. The company's owner tells the employee that this claim wasted his time, and that she would be fired if she ever filed a claim again. She then files another charge with the EEOC, and is fired by the owner. Even if her claims have no merit, the employee now has a strong claim that the employer engaged in illegal retaliation against her.

Defamation

Defamation is a statement that injures the reputation of a third party. In order to prove defamation, a claimant must show that a false and defamatory statement was made to a third party, caused by at least negligent behavior by the party releasing the information, that resulted in special harm to the claimant. For example, an employer discharges an employee and lets it be known within the employer that this was done due to difficult behavior by the person (when this was not actually the case). Making this statement within the employer lowers the former employee's reputation within the business, possibly making it more difficult for him or her to gain references to assist in finding another job. The example notes a possible outcome of a defamation situation, since it can cause damage in the form of reduced job opportunities.

Given the facts just noted, many employers elect to discharge employees without giving any reason at all, thereby allowing them to avoid charges of defamation. However, this lack of communication leaves the employer open to charges of discrimination when the discharged person is a member of a protected group. Also, the discharged person's co-workers have an interest in knowing the reason for discharge, so that they will have more information about what is considered acceptable conduct in the workplace. Consequently, the employer needs to balance the need to distribute discharge information to those who will learn from it, while not broadcasting the information to an excessive degree.

An employer may also need to be concerned about defamation claims when giving references in regard to former employees. When a reference contains false or unsubstantiated information which then causes a person to not obtain a job, that person could make a valid defamation claim against the employer. To avoid defamation claims related to references, some employers have a standard policy of not issuing them at all, or of only issuing basic information, such as the dates of a person's employment with the firm and the position(s) held.

Recovery of Back Pay

When an employer is found to owe back pay to an employee, the employer is required to make up the difference between what the employee was paid and the amount that he or she should have been paid (known as back pay). These situations are usually dealt with as violations of the Fair Labor Standards Act (FLSA). The FLSA provides for recovering unpaid minimum and/or overtime wages by any of the following methods:

- The Wage and Hour Division supervises the payment of back wages.
- The Secretary of Labor can bring suit for back wages.
- An employee can file a private suit for back pay.
- The Secretary of Labor can obtain an injunction to restrain anyone from violating the FLSA, including the unlawful withholding of proper minimum wage and overtime pay.

Employees cannot bring suit under the FLSA if they have been paid back wages under the supervision of the Wage and Hour Division or if the Secretary of Labor has already filed suit to recover the wages.

Generally, a two-year statute of limitations applies to the recovery of back pay. In the case of willful violations, a three-year statute of limitations applies.

Unemployment Insurance Benefits

Each state has its own unemployment insurance program, which evaluates unemployment claims and administers the payment of benefits to individuals. Each of the states has its own rules regarding who is eligible for unemployment benefits, the amounts to be paid, and the duration of those payments, within guidelines set by the federal government.

From the perspective of employment law, the main issue is determining when an employee is disqualified from receiving unemployment benefits. This situation arises when a worker leaves his or her job without good cause, or when the worker engages in misconduct serious enough to be discharged as a result. If a worker files a claim that protests either of these situations, then the state-level department of labor will review the facts of the case and decide whether the individual should receive unemployment benefits.

A state government may allow unemployment benefits in cases where a worker left for good cause, which is usually defined as sexual harassment, compulsory retirement, illness, or military service. These determinations are made at the state level, and vary substantially by state.

A disqualification from unemployment insurance benefits may be tied to a discharge related to misconduct. This is usually due to repeated absences from work, drug use, insubordination, or the violation of the employer's rules. This situation differs substantially from a discharge due to incompetence, where a worker will generally be entitled to unemployment benefits. The charge of absenteeism will depend on its cause; for example, repeated absences due to a family issue may be excused by the state-level adjudicator assigned to the case, whereas a series of unexplained absences might not be.

Termination Decisions

A common allegation is that employees are terminated because they are too old. This can be a discriminatory practice when the terminated employee is in the protected class that is more than 40 years old. In this case, it must be proven that the person's employment was terminated for reasons other than age. An interesting variation on this concept is when a person is terminated and replaced by a person who is younger, but more than 40 years old. In effect, both parties are within a protected class. In this case, age discrimination can still be proven when a replacement is substantially younger, despite also being in a protected class.

Employer Rights

Most of this book has been concerned with how to deal with employee rights. In this section, we address the other side of the equation, which is the rights of the employer.

Employee Duty of Loyalty to the Employer

Employees owe a duty of the loyalty to their employer, which mandates that they work in the best interests of the employer during their term of employment. A particular concern with this issue arises when an employee is preparing to leave the employer and then compete with it. The employee is allowed to prepare for the new activity while still employed by the employer, but cannot actively compete while still working for it. This means that employees can inform customers that they will be leaving the firm, but cannot solicit them for business until after they have left.

Misappropriation of Trade Secrets

A similar situation arises when an employee misappropriates the trade secrets of an employer. A trade secret is something used in an entity's business that (a) is not known or readily accessible by competitors, (b) has commercial value or provides a competitive advantage in the marketplace, and (c) the owner of the information protects it from disclosure through reasonable efforts to maintain its secrecy. Of the requirements stated in this definition, the most essential element is the requirement to take reasonable steps to protect a trade secret. If the employer does so, then it has a valid claim against any employee that misappropriates the secret.

EXAMPLE

Norman wants to set up a competing business. His employer maintains a list of current customers in a password-protected file. Norman figures out the password and then uses the customer list to solicit customers, eventually stealing several away from his employer. Since the employer took steps (the use of password protection) to hide the customer list, the employer has a valid claim against Norman for the misappropriation of trade secrets.

A variation on the concept is the inevitable disclosure doctrine, which states that an employer can seek to enjoin a former employee from working in a job that may result in the use of trade secrets, even though the employer has no evidence that those trade secrets have actually been used. This situation most commonly arises when an employee in a more senior position is hired by a competitor to work in approximately the same job. In this situation, the former employer can make a case that the employee will inevitably use the former employer's trade secrets in his or her new position.

Covenants Not to Compete

When employees have vital and unique information about their employer, the employer may require that they sign a covenant not to compete. In order to be enforceable, these agreements must have a limited duration and cover a specific geographic region. Since these agreements can severely constrain the ability of a person to make a living, a non-competition agreement must be limited in its scope. For such an agreement to be enforceable, it must meet all of the following criteria:

- The employer must be seeking to protect a legitimate interest. This means that the employee must have specialized knowledge that justifies the enforcement of a covenant not to compete.
- The agreement must have a reasonable duration. A two-to-three-year duration is generally considered to be reasonable.
- The geographic reach of the agreement must be reasonable. The region covered should not exceed the area serviced by the current employer. When an agreement contains no geographic limitation at all, then the duration of the agreement will need to be short, such as in the range of six to 12 months.

- The employer is paying adequate consideration in exchange for the agreement. It is usually considered sufficient when the agreement is entered into at the start of a person's employment. Forcing an employee to sign the agreement later on, without some type of compensation boost, may make the agreement unenforceable.

Some employers take the approach of including a covenant not to compete clause in the severance agreements they sign with employees. This approach fulfills the fourth of the preceding requirements for a valid agreement, which is that the employer is providing adequate consideration in exchange for the agreement.

Employee Inventions

An employee may develop an invention while employed by a business, and does so during normal employer working hours and using employer resources. The basic rule is that, when the employer hires a person to design a specific invention, the resulting patent should be assigned to the employer. If the person is not hired in order to design an invention, but does so on employer time and using employer resources, then the employer should be granted a non-exclusive, irrevocable right to use the invention; this is payback for the employer's investment in the development of the product. However, an employer can override the preceding rule by entering into a contract with its employees, stating that employees must assign the rights to all inventions developed using employer resources to the employer. It can be difficult for an employer to enforce a holdover clause in such an agreement, where former employees must still assign their rights to inventions to the employer within a certain period of time after their employment has ended.

The Use of Employment Arbitration

An employer generally wants to avoid lawsuits from employees, since the cost and duration of lawsuits is substantial. A possible alternative is *arbitration*, where both sides agree to let a third party (the arbitrator) reach a decision that is binding on both parties. One advantage of doing so is that arbitration is a much faster process, requiring months rather than years to complete. Also, the cost of arbitration is much lower than the legal fees associated with a lawsuit. However, an arbitrator's fee must be paid in advance, whereas an employee who chooses litigation may employ an attorney under a contingent fee arrangement where there is no up-front cost at all.

A downside of arbitration is that employees can see it as an act of coercion by their employer, especially when the employer requires the use of arbitration as a condition of employment. Another downside from the perspective of the employee is that these arbitration agreements can be skewed to favor the employer so much that they essentially allow the employer to avoid the bulk of all employee claims. Yet another concern is that arbitration does not allow an employee the right to a trial by jury. And finally, judicial reviews of arbitration awards are quite limited; this usually only happens when an arbitrator was clearly biased or corrupt. In all other cases, an arbitration decision is final.

In short, the use of arbitration is unquestionably faster and less expensive than lawsuits. However, the process can be skewed to favor the employer more than the employee, and so can be perceived as being unfair by employees.

Summary

A common theme running through the topics in this chapter is that there are legal issues associated with almost any interaction between an employer and its employees. An employer can elect to deal with these issues only as they arise, but doing so can be expensive, in terms of legal fees and settlements with employees. A much better approach is to discuss employer operations with a labor attorney, who can provide advice about the types of labor issues that are most likely to arise, and the steps that can be taken to prevent them.

Chapter 4
Dealing with Labor Unions

Introduction

A larger workforce may be organized into a union, which represents its interests with the employer. In these cases, union relations form a large part of the efforts of the human resources and legal departments. In this chapter, we provide an overview of the labor union concept, how collective bargaining works, grievances, strikes, how to deal with unions, and several related matters.

The Labor Union Concept

A labor union is a separate entity that represents the interests of a group of employees with their employer. A union may be either a craft union or an industrial union. A *craft union* caters to employees having a particular skill, and may operate an ongoing apprenticeship program to train more people in that skill. An *industrial union* caters to groups of employees, irrespective of their skills. Thus, an electricians' union would only be interested in organizing all of the electricians in a company, while an industrial union would be interested in organizing the entire production staff of the same company.

The goal of a labor union is to improve the wages, benefits, job security, and working conditions of the employees it represents. It does so by negotiating a collective bargaining agreement with management, and then administering the agreement on behalf of the employees it represents. The union also represents union members who have grievances with an employer.

Employees have to vote to join a labor union. The reasons they may have for doing so are varied, but generally include one or more of the following:

- *Compensation.* An employer has a history of paying low wages in comparison to the market, or there is favoritism or obscurity in how pay increases are formulated.
- *Job security.* An employer has a history of terminating the employment of higher-paid employees and replacing them with lower-paid employees. Alternatively, there may be a practice of routinely laying off employees when there is a slight downward blip in sales.
- *Management disconnect.* The management team may treat employees like disposable commodities, rather than with respect. For example, disciplinary actions for being slightly tardy could be severe, such as immediate termination. The management attitude that typifies this issue is, "if you don't like it here, leave."
- *Career path.* Employees that feel stymied by the advancement system within an employer now have the option to be employed within the union, working their way up through its management ranks.

- *Social system.* If an employer does not construct a social environment for its employees, a union will do so instead. Employees may identify more closely with the social activities sponsored by a union than they do with their employer.

If a majority of employees vote in favor of being represented by a union, the union becomes their exclusive representative for the purpose of *collective bargaining.* Collective bargaining is when a union represents a group of employees to negotiate with the employer in regard to their compensation and working conditions. The group of employees being represented is referred to as a *bargaining unit.* A bargaining unit may encompass employees situated in several employer locations, or it may include only a portion of the employees in a single location.

In order for a union to be certified as the official representative of a bargaining unit, the following steps must be completed:

1. *Authorization cards.* At least thirty percent of the employees in a prospective bargaining unit must sign authorization cards that indicate their interest in being represented by a union. A union will typically not continue with additional certification efforts unless it can collect cards from half of the targeted employee group.

2. *Voluntary recognition.* The union may approach management, asking for a card-check election or a neutrality agreement. Under a *card-check election,* the employer accepts a union based on a majority of employees signing authorization cards. Under a *neutrality agreement,* the employer does not oppose the union's organizing activities. Either approach essentially eliminates the opposition of the employer to unionization.

3. *Petition for election.* If the employer does not voluntarily grant recognition of the union, the union sends a petition for election to the National Labor Relations Board (NLRB). The NLRB will then investigate the circumstances to see if the request for election is valid. If so, the NLRB authorizes the conduct of an election within one month.

4. *Election campaign.* An election campaign is conducted, in which the union and the employer represent their cases to the employees located in the prospective bargaining unit. During this campaign, the employer is not allowed to fire employees in order to discourage union activism or to threaten to do so as a result of the outcome of the election. The employer must also post notices in the workplace concerning the date and location of the upcoming election.

5. *Election.* A secret ballot election is conducted by the NLRB. Representatives of the employer and the union watch over the election, and can challenge the eligibility of any voter. If a majority of employees vote in favor of the union, it is certified to represent the bargaining unit, including those employees in the unit that did not vote in favor of union representation. If the vote is tied, the union is not certified.

When a union is certified, this does not mean that the employer must immediately accede to its demands, only that the two parties will bargain in good faith with each other (see the Collective Bargaining section).

Essentially the same process that was just described for certification may also be used to decertify a union. It requires a petition by at least thirty percent of all union members to hold a decertification election; the petition must be received within 60 to 90 days of the end of the current union contract with the employer. If a majority of the union members vote against the union, the union is decertified. A key point is that management cannot initiate or instigate the petition; it must come from the union members.

A labor union is typically organized as a local branch (or *local*), which is affiliated with a national labor union. The national union assists in organizing activities, provides educational resources and training, lobbies at the state and national level, and dispenses strike funds to locals. Most employee interaction is with the local that represents the employee with his or her employer.

Collective Bargaining

Once a union has been certified, the employer and union enter into a bargaining process to create a collective bargaining agreement. This process must be conducted in good faith, which means that both parties advance proposals, make concessions as needed, and provide whatever information is needed to advance the process.

The negotiation of a collective bargaining agreement can be a difficult one. Typically, each side sets a bargaining position that represents its optimum outcome, which can represent a widely diverging set of positions. Each party also has a minimum set of outcomes across its mix of demands that it will agree to – if the negotiations do not reach that minimum position, the parties will be stalemated.

It is possible that either party may make a demand that it knows will be rejected by its counterpart. Such a demand may have been presented as a throwaway, where it is used to offset a demand by the other party, so that neither demand is incorporated into the final agreement. Another reason for issuing such a demand is to begin arguing in its favor over the course of several iterations of the agreement; thus, a demand is introduced and rejected in the current round of negotiations as a signal that the presenting party wants to address this topic, and will do so with increasing vigor over time.

If there is no prospect of reaching an agreement, the union may threaten to go on strike (when employees refuse to work), while the employer may threaten a lockout. These threats may be used to break a deadlock, or they can be serious threats. In the latter case, a mediator may be brought in to act as a facilitator. A mediator cannot force an agreement, but can be useful in re-opening communication channels and finding alternative resolutions.

A different approach is *arbitration*, where both sides agree to let a third party (the arbitrator) make a decision that is binding on both parties. Given the economic impact of an adverse arbitration ruling, there are not many situations in which arbitration is considered a serious alternative. If a union and employer can be convinced to consider arbitration, they will conduct a detailed review of the prior decisions of each possible arbitrator, to detect signs that the person might render a judgment adverse to their interests.

When a contract between a union and an employer is constructed, the bargaining unit must first ratify the agreement. If ratified, the agreement will typically be in effect for a three-year period. If the agreement is not ratified, the union and employer may return to the bargaining table to fashion a more acceptable agreement, which will then be voted on again.

The resulting agreement defines the compensation and conditions of employment to which the parties have agreed. The agreement may contain the following provisions:

- *Wage rates.* States the wages to be paid for each job classification for each year covered by the agreement. A cost-of-living adjustment may also be included, as well as the rates to be paid for overtime, shift differentials, and other forms of pay. A two-tier wage system may be mandated (see the following section).
- *Severance pay.* States the amount of pay that will be issued if an employee is laid off or terminated.
- *Holidays.* States the holidays for which employees will receive compensation.
- *Vacation.* States the formula by which vacation time is earned.
- *Union shop.* The union shop concept states that an employer that has unionized employees must require all new employees hired into job classifications represented by the union to join the union. There is typically a short period, such as one month, when a new hire is not automatically enrolled in the union. After that period has expired, the new hire must enroll, or his employment will be terminated.
- *Agency shop.* Employees are not required to join the union. However, all employees within a bargaining unit must pay dues to the union in exchange for its services in representing them.
- *Open shop.* Employees are not required to join the union; non-members are not required to pay dues to the union.
- *Dues checkoff.* The employer is required to withhold union dues from employee paychecks and forward these amounts to the union.
- *Grievance procedure.* Describes the procedure to be followed when an employee has a complaint about the employer.
- *Employee security.* Describes the order in which employees are laid off and recalled from a layoff, as well as the order in which promotions are determined. The fundamental underlying concept is that those employees with the most seniority have the most security and promotional opportunities.
- *Work rules.* Lays out the rules under which employees can be directed to conduct tasks.
- *No strike/no lockout.* The union agrees not to engage in any strikes during the term of the agreement, while the employer agrees not to engage in any lockouts. Doing so provides economic security to both sides.

- *Reserved rights.* States that any rights not specifically covered in the agreement are assigned to management. This eliminates any arguments over the applicability of any issues not specifically covered by the agreement.

The agreement may also state the rights of the employer, which encompass the determination of the employer's direction, the allocation of resources, and the supervision and performance review of employees.

Once all parties have approved an agreement, those responsible for negotiating its terms on behalf of the employer must then meet with the lower-level supervisors who deal with union members. The intent of these meetings is to explain the terms of the new contract, and how these terms will alter the manner in which the employer deals with those employees covered by the agreement.

During the term of an agreement, issues will inevitably arise that are not covered by the existing agreement, or which are unsatisfactory to one party or the other. These issues usually form the basis for the negotiations associated with the next three-year iteration of the agreement. These issues will be brought to the attention of the union by the *union stewards*, who are the front-line representatives of the union members. Similarly, lower-level supervisors administer the agreement on behalf of the employer, and so will forward suggestions to senior management regarding how the agreement should be adjusted in its next iteration.

The Two-Tier Wage System

In certain sectors of the economy, there has been a continuing decline in the number of employees, due to a combination of lower-priced competition in other countries and excessively high wage rates within the country. Employers have been required to maintain these higher wage rates under their contracts with labor unions. The unions realize how the overseas labor rates are impacting their membership, and so have proved amenable to the concept of the two-tier wage system. Under this approach, newly-hired employees are paid a starting wage that is substantially less than the amount paid to existing employees, though they typically receive the same benefits package. There are variations on the concept, such as only hiring non-essential people at the lower wage rate.

The key benefit of the two-tier wage system is that some jobs have returned to the country, lowering the unemployment level. However, because the lower-tier wage rates are extremely low in some instances, employee turnover has increased, with the reduced levels of morale and productivity that would be expected with lower compensation levels.

Unfair Labor Practices

An unfair labor practice (ULP) arises when an employer or union engages in activities that restrain employees from their rights to organize (in the case of the employer) or coerce them to do so (in the case of the union). The following exhibit contains several instances of unfair labor practices.

Examples of Unfair Labor Practices

Employer Unfair Labor Practices	Union Unfair Labor Practices
The employer interferes with union organizing activities	The union threatens those employees not voting for union certification
Employer management controls the union	The union refuses to bargain with the employer's negotiators
The employer discriminates against those employees who are union members	The union requires the employer to terminate the employment of someone working to decertify the union
The employer does not bargain with the union in good faith	The union charges excessive membership fees

An employer, employee, or a union can file a ULP claim with the NLRB. Once received, the NLRB issues a notification of the claim to the charged party, asking for information about the case. An agent of the NLRB then conducts an investigation, interviewing the impacted parties and issuing a recommendation to the regional director of the NLRB. Possible outcomes are dismissal of a claim, an informal settlement that does not result in a Board order, or a formal settlement that does result in a Board order. These settlement options can be appealed.

> **Tip:** Supervisors may unknowingly commit an unfair labor practice. To reduce these instances, coach them in how to respond to various labor-related scenarios, perhaps assisted by a labor law attorney.

Grievances

When union members have an issue with their employer, they can complain through their union, which is called a *grievance*. The contract between the union and the employer states the manner in which grievances are to be handled. A grievance is normally initiated for one of the following violations of:

- The terms of its contract with the union
- Employer rules
- Employer safety standards
- Working conditions

There are usually several levels through which a grievance can be addressed. The bulk of all grievances involve a simple airing of the problem between the employee and his or her supervisor, with the union steward sitting in on the meeting. If the issue is not settled during this meeting, the issue is documented on a complaint form and handled by higher levels of managers on both sides. This form states the issue, the clause of the contract that has been violated, and the requested resolution. If more senior management cannot settle the issue, it is usually settled through arbitration, where an impartial third party decides upon the outcome.

Strikes

A union can vote to go on strike, where union members refuse to work. There are two types of lawful strikes, which are as follows:

- *Economic strike.* This is when the intent is to improve the compensation, work hours, or working conditions of employees. In this situation, the employer can hire replacement workers, and can legally retain the replacement workers. The employer does not have to rehire strikers if doing so would result in the termination of employment for the replacement workers.
- *Response to unfair labor practices.* If employees feel that the employer is engaging in unfair labor practices, they can go on strike to protest these practices. Under this scenario, the employer can still hire replacement employees, but must rehire the strikers once the strike is concluded.

A strike can also be illegal. This situation arises when workers go on strike despite a no-strike clause in the union contract (known as a wildcat strike), or when there is serious misconduct by strikers (such as physically blocking someone from entering the company premises), or when a strike supports unfair labor practices by the union. A sit-down strike, where employees stop working and remain in the workplace, is also classified as an illegal activity.

Strategy and Tactics: Union Perspective

A union will not necessarily be able to represent all of the workers in a company; instead, it may only be able to unionize a small segment, such as the production workers or the maintenance staff. If so, the optimum strategy for the union is to focus its unionization efforts on those areas of the company in which the prospect of a strike is most likely to impact the entire company. For example, a strike by the maintenance staff of a manufacturing firm will soon impact production, as machines can no longer be repaired. A variation on this approach is to target a key supplier of a major company. If a strike causes the supplier to halt its shipments to the company, the company can exert pressure on the supplier to yield to the demands of the union. Another tactic is to time a strike for when a company is straining to meet high levels of customer demand, since the amount of profits lost is likely to be substantial. The management of such a company may weigh the strikers' demands against the amount of lost profits and decide to accede to their requirements.

An essential strategy for unions to pursue is the elimination of right to work laws. To this end, they support those candidates willing to pursue this goal in states where right to work laws exist. Support can include funding of the campaigns of politicians, as well as getting out the vote to support these candidates. Unions can employ a multiplier effect, where they pressure not only their union members, but also the friends and families of those members to vote in favor of designated candidates.

> **Note:** A *right-to-work law* states that an employer cannot enter into an agreement with a union that requires the employer to force all new hires to join the union. The theory behind these laws is that employees have the right to decide for themselves whether they want to be part of a union. These laws are typically enacted at the state level.

As a general operating concept, a union can cooperate with trade schools to educate workers in specific skills. By doing so, the union is creating a base of young workers who have had a positive experience with it, and who are therefore more willing to engage in unionizing activities at a later date on behalf of the union.

There are also several tactics that unions pursue when they target a company for unionization. These include the following:

- *Salting.* A union can put people through union organizer training, and then encourage them to apply for jobs at a company. If accepted, these people then work from the inside to unionize the workforce. Employers are not allowed by law to terminate these people solely on the basis of their affiliation with the union, though they can be terminated for poor performance, like any other employee.
- *Flooding.* A union targets a company for a unionization drive by bringing a number of union organizers into the community where the company is located. These organizers learn everything they can about the company, with a particular emphasis on those departments where there is employee disaffection, and try to unionize whichever group of employees appears to be most willing to listen.
- *Leaflets.* Leaflets are distributed to employees that state the benefits of joining a union. They can also be used to present counter-arguments to the positions being made by management. This can result in an ongoing series of leaflet distributions.
- *Picketing.* Groups of employees are stationed near the entrance to a business, carrying signs that convey a message to anyone passing through or near that point. The intent may also be to prevent the entry of anyone into the facility.

Once a union has established itself within a company, it can strategize how to approach upcoming contract negotiations with management. One option is to hold a strike vote. Union members can be encouraged to vote in favor of a strike vote before negotiations even begin. By doing so, the union can show that its membership is strongly supportive, which may give management cause to reconsider an aggressive negotiating stance. Other alternatives that can pressure management into signing a favorable agreement are:

- *Sick-outs.* A large number of employees call in sick, thereby slowing down or halting operations.
- *Work slowdowns.* Employees are on-site, but work at a considerably reduced rate, so that productivity levels decline sharply.

- *Boycotts.* Union members and their friends and family do not purchase the company's products. When the local is part of a national union with a massive membership, this can represent a notable decline in sales for the employer.

Strategy and Tactics: Employer Perspective

Company strategies and tactics concerning unions can be enacted before a union ever makes an appearance, or after it is apparent that union organizing activities have begun. These actions fall into the following categories:

Preventive Activities

- *Equitable compensation.* Continually examine the compensation and benefits paid to employees to see how they equate to industry-standard levels. If these levels are low, a union has reasonable grounds for enticing employees with promises to improve compensation.
- *Equitable treatment.* Review any recurring complaints made by employees to see if there are issues that the company should address, perhaps in such areas as safety, break time, and flexible work schedules. If so, consider engaging in some level of accommodation, thereby improving employee satisfaction with the company.
- *Consistent promotion path.* Have a well-designed system in place for advancing employees into higher-paying positions, avoiding any hint of favoritism. Doing so keeps employees from wanting to join a union in order to advance through the union hierarchy instead.

Reactive Activities

- *Solicitation rules.* Enact rules that the company e-mail system, bulletin boards, and other forms of solicitation are only to be used for company business. Doing so makes it harder for anyone to solicit on behalf of a union using company property.
- *Delay.* Unions tend to focus their energies on union certification activities within a short period of time, fomenting as much unrest as possible that peaks on the date of the certification election. If the employer can delay this election, it is more difficult for the union to prolong its organizing activities, resulting in a reduced proportion of votes in favor of certification.
- *Bargaining unit determination.* The company will likely want to minimize the impact of a union on its operations by attempting to limit the size of a bargaining unit. For example, management can argue that professional and non-professional employees should not be combined into a bargaining unit, or that the interests of the proposed members of a bargaining unit are not sufficiently similar.

If the members of a union go on strike, company management may decide to replace the striking workers. By doing so, it can keep operations running, though possibly at a reduced level of effectiveness. If the strike is prolonged, management may decide to permanently replace the strikers with their replacements, especially since the effectiveness of the replacement workers will have improved as they gain experience. Also, the threat of permanent replacement makes it less likely that union members will want to go on strike in the first place. The downside of taking the aggressive stance of bringing in replacement workers is the long-term damage to relations between the company and its union members.

> **Note:** If a strike was initiated over unfair labor practices by the employer, union members must be reinstated at the end of the strike.

A preemptive tactic when a union threatens to go on strike is for the company to engage in a *lockout*. Under a lockout, the employer blocks union members from entering the premises. Replacement workers and managers instead fill in for those employees no longer allowed on the premises. This approach works well when the union does not have a large strike fund with which to reimburse its union members. The concept is particularly effective if the business can be operated with a relatively small number of workers.

Another approach to dealing with a cantankerous union is to build up finished goods inventories in advance of contract negotiations. By doing so, the company sends the message that it is preparing for a strike by having enough stock on hand to continue servicing the needs of customers for a certain period of time. The downside to this approach is the extra cash investment needed to support a higher level of inventory.

Summary

Dealing with a union can be expensive for an employer, given the additional cost of an industrial relations staff, the time required to deal with grievances, and the added cost of union demands for improved compensation and benefits. The best way to avoid these issues is to instill a culture of treating all employees with dignity and respect, so that there is no need for a union to appear that will enforce these principles. Such a culture can only be enforced at the top of an organization, where senior management sets the tone for how employees are to be treated. This is not a simple case of issuing a memo to junior managers, stating how employees are to be treated. Instead, high standards must be set for employee relations, with continual reinforcement from the management team. If not, managers only have themselves to blame when union organizers find fertile ground among employees.

Glossary

A

Adverse impact. The use of apparently neutral selection procedures that have the effect of excluding a disproportionate number of employees based on their age, color, national origin, race, religion, or sex, and where the selection procedures are not job-related.

Affirmative action. A requirement that a government contractor be proactive in ensuring that employment opportunities are not based on various discriminatory factors.

Arbitration. When an impartial third party hears both sides of a dispute and renders a judgment.

At-will employee. An employee who can be terminated at any time and for any reason by an employer.

B

Bargaining unit. The group of employees being represented by a union.

Bona fide occupational qualification. A work condition that allows an employer to waive discrimination requirements.

C

Card-check election. When an employer accepts a union based on a majority of employees signing authorization cards.

Collective bargaining. When a union represents a group of employees to negotiate with their employer in regard to their compensation and working conditions.

Contingent worker. Someone who operates under a short-term employment arrangement.

Craft union. A union that caters to employees having a particular skill.

D

Disparate treatment. Different treatment of job applicants or employees, giving rise to discrimination.

E

Equal employment opportunity. The concept of not discriminating against an employee or job candidate based on a variety of factors.

F

Four-fifths rule. A measurement used to determine whether a selection procedure has an adverse impact on a protected group.

G

Grievance. A formal complaint that is raised by an employee towards an employer within the workplace.

I

Industrial union. A union that caters to groups of employees, irrespective of their skills.

K

Key position. A position that would cause substantial and grievous economic injury to the employer if the employer is forced to restore a previous holder of that position to it.

L

Lockout. The exclusion of employees by their employer from their place of work until certain terms are agreed to.

P

Protected activity. Providing information about incorrect activities being undertaken by an employer, such as concealing material off-balance sheet transactions, underreporting corporate expenses, and circumventing internal controls.

R

Reasonable accommodation. The removal of unnecessary barriers that restrict employment opportunities or prevent a qualified person from completing the essential elements of a job.

S

Salary. Regular compensation paid in a predetermined amount that is not subject to reduction because of variations in the quantity or quality of work performed.

Sexual harassment. When a person in a position of power creates a hostile work environment or attempts to extort sexual favors from other employees.

T

Tangible employment action. A significant change in a worker's employment status.

Term employee. An employee who is only being hired for a limited period of time.

U

Undue hardship. A disability concept, when there would be an excessive burden on an employer to accommodate an employee, which depends on the cost of the accommodation and the financial resources of the employer.

Union shop. A requirement that all new employees be automatically enrolled in a union.

Glossary

Union steward. The local, on-site representative of a union.

Index

www.ingramcontent.com/pod-product-compliance
Lightning Source LLC
Chambersburg PA
CBHW051351200326
41521CB00014B/2535